# THE EMERGENCE OF SHEPHERD NEAME FROM THE EARLIEST DAYS OF BREWING IN FAVERSHAM KENT

## 1100 - 1732

JOHN OWEN

MMXIV

First published in 2014 by
John Owen, Monskmead House, Throwley, Kent ME13 0PF



Typeset in Berkeley LT 10pt by Mickle Print (Canterbury) Ltd, Canterbury, Kent
Printed and bound in Great Britain by Mickle Print (Canterbury) Ltd, Canterbury, Kent

A catalogue record for this title is available from the British Library
ISBN: 978-0-9559997-7-2

## Acknowledgements

My great thanks must go to Jonathan Neame, the Chief Executive of Shepherd Neame Ltd., and to his father, Bobby Neame, past Chairman and now President of Shepherd Neame Ltd.

Jonathan Neame has shown great interest in the history of the business and been unfailingly encouraging to me in the quest to open up its past, as more than an extension of the marketing department. Bobby Neame has spent many enjoyable hours and lunches helping me to understand what the brewing business is about and what are its processes.

My equal thanks must go to my Faversham antiquarian friends, who have transcribed, indexed, interpreted and published long runs of early primary Faversham records. These are source books of original documents from which I have been able to extract freely details, without having always to refer to the originals. The use and interpretation of all these records is however entirely my own.

Patricia Hyde and Duncan Harrington have published The Early Faversham Town Books and associated documents down to 1579; Arden of Faversham and associated documents; Faversham Fines, Faversham Muster Lists, Faversham Hearth Tax Lists and Faversham Manor Rentals down to the 1670s. Peter Tann has just published The Faversham Charters based on the transcripts of David Wright. Michael Frohnsdorff and Jack Long have advised on the early days of the Abbey. Dr Arthur Percival has once again scrutinised my text and made many helpful suggestions.

My thanks must go also to the staff of The National Archives, The Kent Archive Office, or Kent History and Library Centre as it is now called, and the Canterbury Cathedral Archives, who hold most of the original documents quoted.

To Dr Richard Baker of Achievements at Canterbury the layouts of the pedigrees are due.

Other acknowledgements I hope I have made in the footnotes.

Finally, my thanks go to Tim Ashenden and Kayley Middlebrook at Mickle Print of Canterbury, who have once again spent time beyond the calls of duty to organise and print such an attractive volume.

# CONTENTS

# Introduction

Myths and legends cling to most industries. The lack of accessible historical data and the enthusiasm to add antiquity or romance to a chance remark creates instant history. That becomes fact and that is endorsed by marketing literature. Queen Elizabeth slept here, Admiral Nelson paid off his crew here or General Montgomery held a strategic war meeting here, are but a few local examples. The historian has to use rigour, science and some tact to dislodge them.

In 1864 Shepherd Neame and Co. produced an impressive advertising poster. This expensive chromo-lithograph not only showed the new brew house and yard, garlanded with fresh local hops and barley, but carried the text 'Established in 1698'. Reliability was promoted as rooted in wholesomeness, locality and modernity, but at the same time as rooted in tradition. One can imagine Percy Beale Neame, the 28 years old new partner of just two months, grasping at every opportunity to recoup the £18,000 he had invested in this substantially modernised brewery in Faversham. Even then heritage was deemed to have a strong commercial pull: but a myth was born.

The three words 'Established in 1698' lay like a dormant virus in a system. That claim had never been used before and was not repeated for 84 years. It appeared in neither advertising literature nor in patents nor on letter heads nor on bottles nor on transport. It was not recalled in 1898, for a potential 200 years celebration, when the Brewery had just invested in another big programme of modernisation. In June 1874, when Henry Shepherd chaired a dinner to mark the opening of the new store, The Faversham Mercury newspaper quoted him as saying that the Brewery was established in 1596. That date was never used again, despite being closer to fact.

In 1948 the year of the 'establishment' of the Brewery re-emerged. That too was at a critical time. The company was drawing a deep breath of surprise and thankfulness that it had survived at all from the demands of the War as a family business and without the death of any family member. What better celebration than that of '250 Years of Shepherd Neame, Faversham Brewery' ? As with the poster, the celebrations showed that the Company had both a past and a future. Alas, the charming brochure which was printed to commemorate the event accepted without debate 1698 as the date of 'establishment'. That date has been taken as fact ever since.

No reference to the source of the date used in 1864 survives. The date cannot have been found in the Brewery's original title deeds because they rotted away during the Napoleonic Wars, when a mortgagee buried them for safety. It is unlikely that local and national records were the source. It is more likely that a few easily accessible documents, which were then at the Brewery or with the solicitor James Tassell, but which are now lost, mentioned that date which was then taken out of context or misread.

So is that date a fact or a myth? Is the year 1698 significant in the history of Shepherd Neame or is it just a stepping stone date? If that is not the date of establishment is there one? If not did the Brewery emerge from the evolution of the brewing industry in Faversham, into a form of business recognisable today, by a certain date?

Original documentary sources help to answer these questions. Whilst no early corporate records survive, many local and national records do survive and are much more accessible than 65 let alone 150 years ago.

The Faversham Manor Rentals, Town Books, Local, National and Church Tax and other assorted Assessments stretch in near unbroken lines from the 1570s and some from the Middle Ages. When these are read together the names and dates of the past owners and occupiers of most Faversham premises can be extracted. The occupations and wealth of many can be added by using probate records and court documents. This evidence shows that in 1698 The Brewery was already 125 years old. Richard Marsh purchased from the executors of the previous owners an existing brewery which had been operating continuously at 18 Court Street since at least 1573 by the Castlocke family. This is not to say that The Brewery was newly established there in 1573. This at present is the earliest date for which continuous records are available for that address. Others may have brewed there earlier and others were certainly brewing at an adjacent address, within the present wider site, from at least 1507.

Nor is this to suggest that there was a 'date of establishment' of The Brewery, for that is to use a modern concept of company formation. The Castlocke family, who came to Faversham in 1500, were brewers from at least the 1520s, but at as yet unidentified sites. As they either brought the technology of brewing from elsewhere or bought into it or married into it in Faversham, a theoretical date of 'establishment' might be pushed back into the fifteenth century.

Evidence of brewing in Faversham survives from at least the twelfth century but even by the fifteenth century brewing as an industry was largely fragmented and still in its infancy. The early brewers were often women pursuing a domestic industry and later brewers were often merchants in agricultural produce or yeoman for whom brewing was one of several inter related business opportunities. Shepherd Neame Brewery emerged from this late Mediaeval economy but never burst upon Faversham as a fully fledged new brewer.

In the wider context of commercial history, this is an example of how businesses developed from the Middle Ages in a small but prosperous Kent port and town like Faversham. This shows how businesses were formed centuries ago, why they continued and why so many failed; questions as relevant then as today.

In the narrower context of the brewing sector, this is the story of the changing structure of the industry. In the specific context of the development of family businesses, this is the story of commercial competence, demographics, mortality and individual willpower. Often it is the story of sheer good or bad luck.

The survival of Shepherd Neame Brewery however, in whatever context, from at least 1573 makes it without doubt the oldest surviving brewery in England and one of the oldest surviving breweries in the world.

## CHAPTER ONE

# Early Days of Brewing in Faversham: to 1330

The origins of brewing are 'lost in the mists of time' but by at least the early twelfth century brewing was established in Faversham. By the early fourteenth century it was widespread and rooted in the local domestic economy. This was a cottage industry of home production, carried out exclusively by women. Distribution that early appears to have been independent of production. It was through two inns and a very large number of drink sellers. The former catered for visitors and recreation whilst the later probably catered more for the daily needs of locals. The product was a highly variable, unstable and un-hopped ale. From this early market place the brewing sector emerged.

The introduction to these early days of local brewing has to begin in the mud of Graveney Marshes, on the north east edge of Faversham. In October 1970 a remarkable find was made there; the remains of a boat, possibly English, dating to about 900AD, which contained large quantities of hops, both fruits, bracts and bracteoles. 'At first sight this seems most exciting and suggests connections with the supposed Bavarian discovery of hopped beer in the ninth century. However, one must bear in mind that the plant grew wild in Britain before its introduction for cultivation and in common with other plants was used for more than one purpose. Hops were used as vegetables, the long stems were made into rope and the fluffy inflorescences provided an ideal packing material for a fragile cargo'[1]. This may be an entirely random event. It may be evidence of a hop trade, and what that could mean for the development of beer brewing in Faversham, long before any other records survive. However this find is interpreted, deductions will be debated for years.

To return to what can be interpreted, brewing was, and remained until the nineteenth century, so important for one basic reason. It produced a drink, of which the average adult needed one gallon a day, which was sterilised. This was fundamental to health, at a time when pure water supplies were rarely available in a town. Wells were shallow and shared and next to equally shallow privies which drained into them. Diseases of all kinds were rampant and fatal. The drink was also nutritious and food in liquid form. The ingredients of water and malt were basic and the simple process required only a cauldron and a fire. Brewing could be carried out in the home by women as part of the domestic routine. The process was also cheap at a time when wine was too expensive for most and milk was used for making butter and cheese. The basic product, ale, could be strengthened or varied with herbs or spices according to taste. The result was a product whose quality and reliability was variable in the extreme.

The supremacy of English ale, however, was established by at least the mid twelfth century. That of Canterbury was famous and Archbishop Thomas Beckett took presents of ale to the French Court in 1157.

The earliest general reference to laymen brewing in Faversham is before the reign of King Stephen, which pushes origins back to at least the early twelfth century. There are several more general references in the next century but only in 1311 is there a specific reference to brewing in Faversham[2]. This is an Inspeximus[3], or inspection of earlier documents, which relates to taxation of every brewing exposed for sale.

The earliest surviving lists of names of Faversham brewers are for 1327. These are set out in two remarkable tax lists, or Tallages, for the Manor of Faversham.[4] [Table 1] 253 names with their tax due are recorded and are grouped by occupation. They are all women. Here is not only the detailed structure of the brewing sector but the detailed structure of the entire economy of Faversham. From these lists can be drawn the relative importance of everyone named and the relative importance of each sector of trades in the town. We can see the producers and the distributors at work.

In 1327 there were 87 brewsters in Faversham, all of whom were women. Of these 65 were described as wives, hence the common name of ale-wife; 9 were widows; and the remaining 13 were presumably unmarried.

Assuming that the relative productivity of the brewsters was reflected in the tax they paid the structure of the sector begins to emerge. The wife of Robert de Sillgrave paid more tax than anyone else at 5/-; the wife of William ate Forstalle paid 4/6d and 7 other brewsters paid 4/- each in tax. The average tax paid was 1/9d. The lowest brewster paid tax of 6d. The highest tax was 10 times the lowest tax paid but neither varied more than three and a half times from the average.

This suggests that the trade was well spread but there was a handful of bigger producers probably using more than small domestic kitchen equipment.

There are no production details but an estimate of production output can be attempted from these figures. Assumptions of the probable have to be made. The first is that all brewing was taxed whether put up for sale or not. The second is about population. Assume that the population of Faversham was 1500[5], of which 1000 were adults and 500 children, and assume that average daily consumption per adult was 1 gallon per day[6] or 365 gallons per annum and of children half that. The brewsters annual output would have been 365,000 gallons or 10,000 barrels for adults plus 2,500 barrels per year for children. To this must be added the consumption of travellers along the London Road, traders coming into the town for the weekly markets from the villages and mariners using a busy Creek. If the population is assumed to have increased by 5% per week an additional 600 barrels per year have to be added. A total output of approximately 13,000 barrels per annum may have been needed to meet local consumption.

This can be allocated to quartiles of brewsters. The nine largest tax payers contributed 25% of the total tax paid[7] so this group possibly produced 3250 barrels per year or about 360 barrels per annum each, or an average of 7 barrels per week each. The lowest quartile of brewsters, who paid one tenth of the tax, may have brewed therefore only a 1/2 barrel per week. The first would supply the weekly needs of 36 people, or 9 households, and the lowest those of only 2 or 3 people, barely a household. The production of even 6 barrels per week suggests that for the top quartile of producers brewing had become more than a home kitchen operation. Their production was for more than the consumption of the household or immediate neighbours. At the lowest end production was barely above subsistence level.

In addition to brewing by the townspeople there was independent brewing by the Abbey of Faversham after 1148. All monastic foundations had to provide for the well-being of the monks, the laymen attached to the abbey and visitors. The very first buildings to have been completed, and to have been kept in good working order, would have been the bake house, the malt house and the brew house.[8] These were usually sited on the perimeter of the outer courtyards of monasteries, to avoid the spread of fire, and near a well. The exact site of the Faversham Abbey brew house is unknown but it was probably on the north west side of the outer yard, behind what is today 60 Abbey Street. This area was known as Well Orchard after the Reformation, probably because of the well, which was discovered in the nineteenth century, nearby.[9] The well would have been critical to the production of quality ale.

The twelve monks who came from Bermondsey probably had a brewer among them to establish the plant. If not lay brothers or an experienced brewer from the town would have been employed.

With production needed to sustain the Abbey, the brew house would have been the largest, and given the early wealth of the Abbey, probably the most sophisticated one in Faversham at that time. The output would have been also larger than that of any town brewster for some time. Twelve brothers, probably as many lay brothers/workers and possibly as many visitors per week, who would have drunk at least one gallon of ale each per day,[10] would have consumed one barrel of ale per day or 365 barrels per annum.

Distribution of brewing output in Faversham is also recorded in the Tallage. This is the earliest surviving record of the way ale was sold in the town. The lists and names of the distributors follow those of the brewsters. They are grouped under Innkeepers or Tipplers. There are 2 inn keepers and 66 tipplers or drink sellers. Men predominate here; there are only 2 wives, 2 widows and 1 women, presumably unmarried. The distribution of ale was very local, as it did not travel well nor last long. Ale export was rare. The export from Kings Lynn, Norfolk, to the Continent in the thirteenth and fourteenth centuries was the exception.

The relative importance of the distributors is probably reflected in the tax paid. The two inn keepers paid 4/- and 1/- respectively; or an average of 2/6 each. They were at the top end of tax payers. The tipplers paid an average of 8 1/2 d each, with the highest amount paid of 3/- and the lowest of 4d. The difference between the highest and lowest was 12 times, little different from the brewsters. By 1327 a public house trade was established in Faversham.

The size of the distributors appears more polarised than the size of the producers. Only three people paid more tax than 1/6. Thomas de Brenle, an inn keeper, paid 4/-; William Carpenter and Richard Beale, both tipsters, paid 3/- each in tax. Henry de Ewelle paid 1/6 and the remainder paid between 4d and 1/- each. There was clearly a range and quality of sales outlets. The two inns and three 'public houses' were at the top end of the market and probably catered for travellers as well as locals. They were recreational centres as well as distributors of a necessity of life. At the lowest end the distributors probably never kept drinking houses but simply sold the necessity direct to neighbours and friends.

It is tempting to speculate which were the inns and the three 'public houses'. The only houses described as inns, two and a half centuries later, were the Ship and the Queens Arms in the central Market Place, but the Bear, which unlike the others had no rear access or yard, was recorded from the 1480s. The other two could be any of the larger houses which survived into the sixteenth century or they may have disappeared by then. [Table 5].

Further deductions can be made about both the brewsters and the inn keepers. Of the brewsters 65 are described as wives and of these the occupations of 18 husbands are recorded. In other words for 25% of the women, brewing was not the main source of family income. For the remaining

75% of the women, brewing was the sole source of family income. As their husbands were not listed as occupied they may have been unemployed or infirmed. Of the occupied husbands 5 were bakers, so the wives of 50% of the bakers were brewsters. Here is a trade which used the same ingredients as for ale; yeast, barley and malt. One can only conjecture how these operations interacted. Of the remaining husbands 8 were butchers, 2 were tanners, 1 was a cryer, 1 was a fisherman and one was an innkeeper.

The relict of Randolphe Note is especially interesting, for she is listed as both an innkeeper (1 of only 2) and a brewster. She was both producing and selling through her own tied house. As she was a widow she may have inherited her husband's inn, which as a brewster she must have supplied. This is Faversham's earliest example of the victualler brewer who was so significant in the mid seventeenth century. The relative tax shows that her brewing was more important than her inn keeping.

The Tallage also helps to recreate the commercial topography of the town. The most startling statistic is that every third house was brewing for sale and every fourth house was a drink selling establishment. At least every other house was brewing or distributing ale. The major brewsters must have used good water supplies so were probably not situated in the central Market Place, with all the water contamination that implied. They were probably in Court Street, Preston Street and West Street, where the brewers were by the sixteenth century. The lesser ones were probably spread around the town in the cheaper sites with variable water supplies. The major distributors were probably centred round the Market Place. The others were spread likewise through the town.

This in outline is the brewing sector of Faversham in 1327, but what part did this play in the wider economy of the town and port? How important was brewing compared to the other occupations of the town?

In 1327 253 people with occupations were listed. These can be grouped into 233 households. The names are listed under eight occupations. There are 87 brewsters; 2 innkeepers; 66 tipplers; 9 tanners; 15 fishermen; 28 butchers; 10 bakers; and 33 cryers or sellers at windows, the predecessors of shop keepers.

The predominant sector in both terms of numbers and tax, and by assumption, of turnover and/or profitability, was brewing. Over 60% of the taxable, i.e. productive, population of Faversham was directly involved in the production and distribution of ale. Of the total tax paid over 50% was derived from the brewsters and 16% from tipplers and innkeepers. 66% of the tax was derived from the brewing sector. This suggests that this was the most important part of the economy of the town by far.

The next largest sector was that of the shop keepers, or cryers and sellers at windows, who accounted for 13% of the productive population of Faversham. They were followed by the butchers, who accounted for 11% of the productive population. They were followed by the bakers who accounted for 4% of the productive population. These were followed by 15 fishermen and 9 tanners who accounted for 10% of the productive population.

The ranking of turnover and/or profitability, as represented by average taxation per person, is slightly different. Innkeepers come first at 2/6, followed by bakers, followed closely by the brewsters at 1/9. Then there is a sharp fall to the tanners, fishermen and the shopkeepers at 1/-. At the lowest end of the turnover scale are the butchers and the tipplers at 9d each.

The non brewing tradesman were probably also spread around the town but with the largest tax payers concentrated around the Market Place. The tanners were in Tanners Street, with the water running to the west and the fishermen would have been in Abbey Street and West Street. This is the snapshot of the economy of a small Kentish port and town by 1327.

Evidence from other towns suggests that this socio-economic profile was common at this date. In 1287 a Tallage of Leicester recorded 116 brewsters part of a town total of 405[11]. Here 30% of the working population was brewing. Closer to home at Maidstone in 1386 106 women were named as brewsters part of about 350 households[12]. A similar percentage was brewing.

The importance and scale of brewing both socially and economically led to regulation and taxation of the sector. These can be traced from very early days in Faversham.

The protection of the consumer of bread and ale, the basis of diet in mediaeval days, is the earliest form of consumer protection known. The development of the system of an Assize of Bread and Ale attempted to ensure minimum standards of quality and to control price.

At first this was possibly a royal jurisdiction but came to be operated and enforced by the manorial court. It was endorsed by national legislation from time to time. In Faversham the King exercised these rights until 1141 and from then until 1147 by William of Ypres as the lord of the manor. With the founding of the Abbey, and the passing of the lordship of the manor to the Abbot of Faversham, these rights passed to him.[13] The abbot's jurisdiction was confirmed in charters of 1227 and 1279,[14] but only after it had been challenged. In 1356 the Town claimed exemption again from the abbot's jurisdiction.[15]

In the Faversham re-issue of the 1215 Magna Carta, in 1300, national standard measures were set out in Clause 25. 'One measure of wine, ale and corn throughout England shall be the Quarter of London'.[16] The national Assize of Bread and Ale c.1266/7 was another attempt to control the quality and price of these goods,[17] which were predicated on a sliding scale of grain prices.

The enforcement of the Assize had as much to do with consumer protection as it did with the raising of revenue through fines from infringement. Ale-Conners were appointed for different streets in Faversham[18] to taste all ale that was freshly brewed commercially. They could levy fines and fix prices for short measure or poor quality. The fines were paid to the Abbott. In Maidstone many women were fined at monthly sessions of the Portmote for brewing against the Assize. This was more a technical offence that constituted a rudimentary system of licensing.[19] In Chester, however, in 1086 the penalty for making bad ale was the cucking-stool.[20]

The other flow of revenue was through taxation of ale, once again received by the Lord of The Manor of Faversham, the Abbot. Before the foundation of the Abbey this tax of one penny or 'gavel penny', was levied on every brewing exposed for sale. It was possibly paid originally to the church but in 1148 it was granted to the Abbot.[21] Here it remained, but the right to levy it was undermined either by the town over two centuries, or the Abbot needed a fixed cash flow. By 1311 not only had it risen to 1 1/2d but ' The Abbot and Convent remised their right to the custom of Gavelsestre, viz. of receiving 1 1/2d for every brewing (inter alia), to the men of the Commonality of the town of Faversham'. For this, and other concessions, they granted the Abbot a yearly rent of £10.[22] Nothing changed as the town continued to levy a tax, re-named a 'Fine', upon Faversham brewers, totalling £4 per annum, for nearly another 400 years. That is until the costs of collecting it outweighed its fixed value.

The quality and strength of the sole product, ale, would have been extremely variable with so many producers and different ingredients. The quality of malt, one of the basic ingredients, was uneven. Brews contained more oats than barley or the grains were mixed. Herbs or spices were often added and malt was often used two or three times.[23] The ale was much sweeter than continental brews. The depth of wells and hence quality of water was critical to a good brew. However, the ale of Kent was reported as 'superlaively good', according to Gerald of Wales at Christ Church Canterbury in the 1230s.[24] Despite that ale was still a short lived and highly unstable product.

Malting, fundamental to brewing, was as ancient as brewing itself but there are few early references to it. Barley was grown in and around Faversham and there is evidence of malting in the surrounding villages for 1283/5. On the Manor of Boughton 'the men of the open marshes at Sidelands had to provide one man for malting' to the Lord of the Manor, the Archbishop of Canterbury. On the Manor of Charing 'the tenants of Five Acres had to make 20 seams of malt for the Archbishop. On the Manor of Teynham 'men owe work in malting' and 'the cottars are to make as much malt as they can'.[25] Similar obligations no doubt attached to the Abbot's Manor of Faversham, but malting must have been widespread in the town to supply the brewsters. How concentrated this industry was is unknown.

This is the brewing sector in Faversham up to the middle of the fourteenth century. It is a snapshot in time, static and not dynamic, based largely upon one document that has survived miraculously. The evidence of how the sector developed to that position does not exist. However, the sector by 1327 was widespread, fragmented and domestic in character. Here at least is a springboard from which to determine changes in the following centuries.

## CHAPTER TWO

# The Emerging Brewing Industry in Faversham: 1330-1500

In the fifteenth century the brewing sector, in both Faversham and South East England, underwent significant changes at the top end, yet underlying traditional practices continued for centuries more. Changes were incremental but the results were permanent.

The structure of the industry gradually shifted from the fragmented production of the ale wives to a more consolidated production by fewer male professional or 'common brewers'. These were men who became small industrialists of status in the community. Side by side with these, home production for family and friends did continue in many houses, especially in the countryside. Distribution through inns and ale houses, which can be identified and located, became more concentrated. Traditional regulation remained and was reinforced from time to time both nationally and locally. Per capita consumption changed little as there was no cheap substitute to a sterilised brew. Drinking ale or beer remained a necessity of life not an exclusively recreational pursuit. The major change was in the product. By the end of the period ale was being replaced by the hop based beer.

The rate at which the numbers of ale wives contracted and were replaced by brewers can only be estimated as no document like the 1327 Tallage survives for the period. For the century after 1327 not one name of a Faversham brewer, man or woman, has yet been discovered. Only from the 1440s have individuals names survived. These are simply chance and random survivals which are not part of a serial. Thereafter four or five names survive for approximately every twenty five years.

In 1450 there were five names: William Barbour, Richard Brayton, John Orwell, Simon Orwell and John Seyncler.[26] In 1474 William Thornton was named as a brewer.[27] That they were all described as brewers suggests that whilst they may have carried out a range of commercial activities, such as maltsters or corn merchants like later brewers, their main commercial interest was brewing. Later in the century Simon Warmecourt, and possibly Simon Orwell and Nicholas Warnecourt, were also brewing. [Table 2]. None of them were called beer brewers.

In Canterbury by comparison, which was three times the size of Faversham, between 1400 and 1450 12 brewers are identified and between 1451 and 1500 13 are identified. Of these 3 were beer brewers, in 1477, 1489 and 1494.[28]

Some of the Faversham names provide evidence of the earliest examples of succession in a brewing operation and continuation of brewing at the same address for more than one generation. It must be more than coincidence that William Barbour a brewer, John Roger and Nicholas Wyndout transferred their premises to John Orwell, another brewer in 1463.[29] Those premises were 15-17 Preston Street, which continued to be owned by Faversham brewers for two hundred years until the late seventeenth century.[30] In 1474 William Thornton acquired 'a messuage with curtilage and three brewing vessels with appurtenances in Preston Street' from Richard Long, Richard Ledemede and Thomas Rede which they had from John Orwell of Faversham. This too probably refers to 15-17 Preston Street.

Warnecourt is another example. A Warnecourt was a tenant of the Manor of Davington in premises between 2-6 Preston Street, which were described as a brewhouse. There were several subsequent brewing owners but by the mid-seventeenth century the premises were described as a malthouse.[31]

Business relationships or at least friendships of the early brewers are also suggested in their wills. John Orwell was a witness to the will of Nicholas Warencourt and Lawrence Stranshin was a witness to the will of Simon Warmcourt.

These were all men of substance. Simon Warncourte owned 73-74 Preston Street, that fine late mediaeval house. John Seyncler was described as an Esquire in 1450 and may have been also the lawyer and occupier of Graveney Court. William Barbour was described as a Gentleman in 1450. Simon Orwell, who died in 1475/6, had messuages and land in Faversham, Oare, Luddenham, Davington and Preston and amongst other bequests left money for a chalice to be made for his father's church. He also left ' visselles belonging to Brewers Croft' attached to a messuage in West Street.[32] John Orwell clearly had business interests outside the immediate town, for he brought a bill of costs against James Godd of Faversham, who had sued him in the foreign, ie. outside the Liberties of the Cinque Ports, in 1463.[33]

Most of the early identified brewers were active in local government. John Seyncler was a mayor four times between 1438 and 1448. Richard Brayton was a mayor in 1436, 1445 and 1456.

William Barbour was mayor in 1441, 1463 and 1466.The Orwells were mayors in 1437, 1462 and 1466. John Orwell was active at Cinque Ports meetings. He attended Brodhulls at Romney in 1464 and in 1466, when he was a party in a suit to 'conserve the liberty'. He attended there as a Deputy for Faversham in 1472.[34]

Occasionally we have a glimpse of their private lives. In 1450 Jack Cades Rebellion was led from Kent. It was unlike The Peasants Revolt, of a century earlier, as the leaders were merchants, gentlemen and men of substance; not a rabble. The followers entered the City of London to present 25 grievances, against his ministers, to the King. General pardons were granted to many followers amongst whom for Faversham were William Barbour, John Seyncler, Richard Brayton, John and Simon Orwell.

Just as the structure of the brewing sector was changing so was the product. The introduction of hops and hopped ale or beer was the greatest change of all. Faversham was drinking beer from at least 1394. The references are oblique but are repeated in the Corporation minutes in 1448 and again in 1509. In 1394 the Town Presenters are to ensure ' not less than a quart of the best beer or ale is sold for a penny'. In 1448 and repeated in 1509 orders to the Town Porters refer to 'vessels of ale and beer'. Alas neither brewers names, locations nor productions are listed. However, it is inconceivable that with the close contacts between the Low Countries and London that the changes in Faversham did not follow those in the other Cinque Ports and in London.

From the 1370s merchants along the southeast coast and London were importing beer from the Low Countries. In 1393 beer was arriving in Winchelsea.[35] In the late fourteenth century Great Yarmouth, the port with very close connection through the herrings market with the Cinque Ports, was importing between forty and eighty barrels of beer per month.[36]

Imported beer was probably drunk at first primarily by Flemish aliens but it was a small step to them establishing breweries in England. Soon they dominated the beer brewing industry. In 1483 a special assessment of alien beer brewers was imposed.[37] Three were in the Cinque Ports and eight were in London. Giles Beerbrewer in Sandwich was taxed as an alien beer brewer in 1439-1440.[38] By 1441 beer brewing was so widespread that regulation was introduced.[39]

Native beer brewing followed. Fordwich, by 1482, was one of the first Kent towns to have a native beer brewery.[40] William Maycott, the brewer there, may have been related to the Faversham Maycotts. In 1469 John Kyng was beer brewing in Sandwich.[41] In 1476 Robert Mote at Canterbury was described as a beer brewer. By the late fifteenth century beer breweries were well established in London and most towns had beer breweries.[42] It is unlikely that Faversham was any different.

The spread of beer brewing was slower than should have been expected considering that it had a number of advantages over ale. Its greatest advantage was that it was much cheaper to produce than ale, once the more sophisticated equipment was set up. Hops were cheaper than barley and hops produced more drink from much less grain.[43] Hops helped to stabilise the drink, so that it lasted longer, but beer was more bitter than the sweet English ale.

The result was that it became more economic to brew beer on a larger scale than ale. That in turn encouraged the introduction of larger breweries, which needed more capital. As few women had that they were gradually pushed to the margins of production. The marginally profitable ale trade had attracted previously little investment.

Two other factors promoted the beer brewing in Kent. Military provisioning of the armies operating in France and especially the provisioning of Calais by private contractors relied upon big supplies. These cannot all have been provided by London. The second factor was the provisioning of ships crews using the busy Kent ports. Beer lasted longer on voyages than ale. It was the ideal drink for ships crews.

Hops, the new ingredient to the brew, are known to have been imported to England in the 1420s.[44] By the middle of the century they were imported to Rye and Winchelsea. The trade was at first dominated by aliens from the Low Countries. In 1441 and 1442 thirty hods of hops were sold by fifteen such merchants in London to three brewers.[45] English hop gardens were well established in East Kent by the mid sixteenth century[46] but earliest locations are as yet elusive. The earliest Faversham hop garden cannot yet be located before 1590.

During the fifteenth century the names of inns and ale houses in Faversham emerge. That is not to say they originated then but that they are identifiable then. The Bear in Market Place is mentioned in the will of Richard Thornbury in 1488.[47] The Crowne at 114 West Street and the Anker at 25 Court Street are both mentioned in the will of Thomas Reade in 1503/4.[48] These were substantial establishments owned by men of wealth. They owned them but did not operate them. They were investment properties which they leased them to the publicans. This pattern continued for centuries.

Regulation of the sector was both national and local, and of quality, quantity, price and distribution. In 1441 the King granted to Richard Lounde and William Veysy 'the correction, search and survey of all beer brewers in England, by themselves or by deputies' to enforce the Assize of Bread and Ale.[49]

In 1394 Faversham Presenters or Overseers were appointed to present anyone selling less than a quart of the best beer or ale for one penny. Moving beer and barrels around the town was also highly regulated. Town porters not brewery employees had to be used. The Corporation set out the terms in 1448. The brewer and the tappster, or publican, paid one penny each, to the Corporation, for the delivery and collection of each barrel.[50] Even the loading of vessels was regulated. In 1447 Orders were given to the Town Porters concerning the charges for using the town crane. The Porters were to charge 12 pence for every tonne of wine wound up and 1/2 penny for every quarter of malt wound down into the hold.

In Faversham in 1436 the Corporation tried to standardise the size of barrels used by brewers at 30 gallons and 15 gallons for a kilderkin. The fine for failure was 15/- and the barrel was forfeited. Brewers had to use barrels with coopers marks on them. If they held less than the standards a fine of 20/- was paid and imprisonment followed.

During the fifteenth century a new structure of the brewing sector in Faversham was emerging. The sector was consolidating into a limited number of big producers, albeit that domestic production continued for centuries. The industry was becoming male dominated. Distribution through identifiable houses was emerging. Regulation of quality and price was continuing. The biggest change was in the product. Hopped beer was replacing English ale.

## CHAPTER THREE

# The Brewing Families of Faversham: 1500 to 1600

The brewing sector that was becoming established in the fifteenth century became more clearly developed in the sixteenth century. The first feature of the period is of breweries that survived with a continuous family or partnership succession over long periods and on the same site. The second feature is the change in product from un-hopped ale to hopped beer. The third feature is the growth of identifiable inns and ale houses, which also lasted over long periods, and some of which were loosely tied to brewers. The fourth feature of this period is the leading part in local civic life these successful brewers played.

Taking the supply side of the brewing sector first, four groups of producers are evident. At the top end are the town brewers, referred to as common brewers, who brewed for commercial sale and distribution. Next came the victualler brewers, who brewed for their inns or ale houses and possibly small scale local distribution. Next came the home brewers, who brewed for their own domestic consumption. Finally came the foreign brewers whose products were imported to Faversham for commercial distribution. In addition was the brew house of Faversham Abbey, supplying the monks and visitors. The market was not static and the relative importance of these producers changed inevitably during the century.

During the sixteenth century twenty eight Faversham brewers can be identified. [Table 2].[51] Of these, fourteen were major producers, nine were transitory or minor producers and the remainder were servants of the larger producers and occasionally brewers on their own account. From 1500-1525 there were two major brewers and one other; from 1525-1550 there were two major brewers and one other; from 1550-1575 there were five major brewers and six others; and from 1575-1600 there were six major brewers and five others.[52] From this evidence a hierarchy of breweries begins to emerge.

Three brewing families predominated; Castlocke, Stransham and Cole. The Castlockes, about whom nothing is known until they migrated to Faversham, probably from the Isle of Sheppey in 1499, became the leading brewing dynasty in Faversham and established the brewery which emerged ultimately in 1864 as Shepherd Neame and Co. The Stranshams, who are reputed to have originated in Gloucestershire,[53] were established as Faversham commoners by 1466, became brewers but withdrew from brewing by 1583. Thomas Cole, was the largest brewer in Faversham in the 1570s and 1580s and by marriage was related to both the Castlockes and the Stranshams. Through the fortunes of these three families one can see how businesses operated in the sixteenth century and, more interestingly, why they continued or disappeared.

John Sheppey, or John Castlocke as he became known, was appointed Abbot of Faversham in 1499, probably in his early twenties. 'He was a man of business who was called in to retrieve Faversham Abbey from bankruptcy. In 1535 he knew so well every acre of the Abbey estates that he could still direct his agents to keep them productive'.[54] With him came his younger brother, William Castlocke. Clearly he was an entrepreneur with an eye for a chance. The connections and entres to the merchants of the town, that the status of his brother the abbot gave, ensured he would not have been treated as any new comer to a town, ie. one who had to work his way up. His was a high entry point.

By 1525 William was a merchant 'importing various goods and exporting beer'.[55] In 1541 William was described as a brewer, when with William Belke junior, barber of Faversham, he 'loaded two hoys of Flushing with grain bought of John Goldfinch of Faversham, which was restrained by the King, and he was bound to deliver it at Dover.'[56] He may have had a formal role in the life of the administration of the Abbey, as his brother was appointing laymen to posts.[57]

What we do not know is where William acquired training as a brewer. Unless he had received a brewing apprenticeship in Sheppey, which is unlikely due to the poor quality water, he must have joined or taken over an existing brewery in Faversham. It is possible that he gained experience at the abbey brew house, but no evidence survives to support this. It is also possible that he was a master rather than a professional craft brewer.

After the Dissolution of the Abbey in 1538 Abbot John enjoyed a comfortable existence. He was allowed to rent a cottage with nine acres in the Abbey grounds and was paid an annual pension of £66.13.4.[58] He died intestate in 1543. He was clearly a man of property, as the administration of his estate was undertaken by his brother William and another townsman, Joseph Beverly, who was in turn MP for Dover and Winchelsea. They were bound in 100 marks (£66), a very large sum, to produce an inventory.[59] William as his closest relative was probably the sole beneficiary. He become an increasingly prosperous townsman.

William died in 1550, also intestate, which suggests that his wife was dead and that he had only one heir. One administrator was a Canterbury inn holder, Radulph Ordymer, who was a Freeman of Canterbury and described as a yeoman in 1542.[60] This suggests a trading relationship beyond Faversham. The main administrator of his estate was his son called John, who was described as a beer brewer.[61] This is the earliest known use of the term in Faversham.

Very little is known of the brewing activities and life of John Castlocke I. Even his dates are uncertain. He was probably born about 1510 and as he disappeared from the town records by 1557 probably died then.[62] Likewise there is no evidence for what happened to his brewing interests. His son, John Castlocke II, was then only five or six so unable to take over a business. Possibly his widow carried it on and remarried. Whatever happened the family tradition of brewing survived, for in 1573 John Castlocke II emerged as the occupier of 18 Court Street[63]: the address from which the business has continued ever since.

John Castlocke II was born about 1552[64] and died in 1613. He built up a flourishing business over a lifetime, which he either re-started or took over at the age of 21. After the death of Thomas Cole in 1593 he became the leading brewer in Faversham. He was a beer brewer for forty years. By 1600 the succession was secured, with his eldest son John Castlocke III working in the business.[65]

The second leading brewing family in Faversham in the sixteenth century was the Stransham family. Lawrence Stransham was born here or in Stalisfield or Lenham before 1472 and had become well established in Faversham by 1500. In 1511 he was described as a brewer, but no details of his background or training survive.[66] In 1512 he was committed to the Fleet Prison for refusing to take the mayoral oath before Abbot Castlocke. He cannot have stayed there very long for in 1516 he was being sued for debt in Chancery.[67] He is described then as a yeoman of Faversham. He died after 1516[68] and before 1532[69] but he took no further part in town politics and left no will or administration. As with the Castlockes in the 1550s the fate of the brewing business and the immediate succession is unknown. None of his four children was old enough to take it over in 1516 but the business either survived or was rebuilt later by his son.

His eldest son, George Stransham, became a successful brewer. He was born about 1510 and is first mentioned in the Faversham Wardmote Book in 1539.[70] That he was elected a Commoner in 1540 shows he was becoming commercially successful and his election as mayor of Faversham in 1562 shows that he had arrived. He died in 1576. His will is interesting as it sets out how he had planned the succession to his brewery. 'Richard Stransham my son and Alice his wife shall have the preferment of the occupation and use of the said brew house and the implements belonging thereto as he now has the same at my hands'.[71] His will also shows what a prosperous townsman he had become. He leased Ospringe and Preston Parsonages and had an interest in Perry Farm. He had rebuilt Ospringe Parsonage house. His two brothers were both Faversham Commoners and Jurats,[72] so his family at that time was embedded in the life of Faversham.

Richard Stransham was the third son of George and one of his eight sons and three daughters. His eldest brother, Thomas, was a lawyer, at Clements Inn then at Doctors Commons. His next elder brother Robert was a Fellow of All Souls Oxford and Secretary to the Earl of Pembroke but in 1604 he is described as Gentleman of Ospringe.[73] He came back to home to end his days. It was Robert who acquired the Parsonages and also left a 'brew house, malt house and mill house at The Standard let to Gabriel Belke for £20 pa.' Another, younger, brother was also a Fellow of All Souls and another brother became a Roman Catholic priest. His three other brothers removed to Maidstone and Sittingbourne. They all moved away from brewing, the source of their wealth.

Richard Stransham was a beerbrewer but at his death in 1583 he is described as a gentleman.[74] He left his property in trust for his wife to sell for the benefit of their son Thomas, who was only nine when his father died. Thomas never became a brewer but became a lawyer of Middle Temple and died unmarried in London. The family became too prosperous or gentrified to remain as brewers; a process epitomised by the grant of arms to Thomas.[75] The senior lines became examples of an upwardly mobile provincial merchant family of the sixteenth century. It was for the husband of Richard's youngest sister, Barbara, who was married to Thomas Cole, to carry on the main brewing business, but by purchase not inheritance.

Thomas Cole is the third leading brewer of Faversham in the sixteenth century. Unlike the Castlockes and Stranshams he did not come from a known local brewing family. Whilst a John Cole endowed The Faversham Grammar School in 1527 there is little record of a Cole family in Faversham during the early part of the century.[76] In 1567 he paid a fine 'for being made free' ie gained his freedom to work in Faversham, and in the following year he is listed as a chamberlain.[77] He first appears in the street lists of inhabitants in 1570.[78] In 1574 he married Barbara Stransham. From her family he purchased his brewery. In his will he refers to... 'my brew house with all the vessels of brewing to the same belonging...which I lately purchased of Robert Streynsham gentleman.'[79] By the time he died in 1593 he was able to leave between £80 and £40 to each of his daughters. He was a new-comer but a successful one.

Thomas Cole did not leave a brewing family to take over his business. He had seven daughters and no sons. The brew house and vessels were left to his wife and after her death to his four daughters. Whilst the premises went to them, the business was carried on by his servant, William

Tomlyn, until 1619.[80] Thomas Cole's youngest daughter, Bennett, was the only one who married a brewer, John Castlocke, whom she married in 1596, but she did not carry any part of the business to him.

One other brewing business, although not one continued by family succession, is recorded in Faversham, on the same site, within 2/7 Preston Street, for the second half of the sixteenth century.[81] The brewers were Thomas Tenacre who died about 1560; William Maycott who died about 1569; and possibly John Finch, related by marriage to Maycott, who died about 1575. Thomas Tenacre may have had several brewing interests. In 1559 Thomas Greenstreete acquired from Thomas Teneker and his wife Magdalen, two messuages, one of which was called The Brewhouse, near the north part of Hynxhyll Lane, now called Cross Lane.[82] There is no record of how the business was transferred, but these men were, like the others, substantial townsmen.

One other brewing family needs mention, not least because of their very long association with the commerce and industry of Faversham until the late nineteenth century. That was the Hilton family. William Hilton is first listed as a brewer in Faversham in the 1580s and appears in West Street in 1583.[83] His activities were modest then but his successors did inherit the Castlocke brewery in 1652.

These were the leading brewing businesses, for which there is an identifiable succession over a long period, but there was at least one other possible brewer of importance in the sixteenth century, albeit not a known founder of a lasting businesses.

Robert Withiot, who came to Faversham in 1474,[84] is recorded as holding ' a tenement called Le Brewhouse next to Gorewell Lane, now Partridge Lane, in 1507.[85] Whilst he was a substantial townsman there is only one other reference linking him to brewing.

Of the handful of other brewers known there are only fleeting references, which suggest that their businesses were modest. There is a single reference to a Michael Hester in 1517.[86] There is a single reference to a John Chantrell, late of Gloucester, in 1527.[87] Cornelius Dowman, probably a Fleming, is listed as a brewer from 1562 to 1584.[88] Clement Oldfield is listed in 1574 only as a brewer. Fowler Derelove was a brewer in the 1580s.[89] John Perte was a brewer in 1571.[90] Richard Huttchyne brewed from 1583 to 1591.[91] Michael Join was described at his burial as a brewer in 1593.[92] None of these were substantial townsmen and none left a business that survived their deaths.

Just as there was a hierarchy of brewers so there was a directly related hierarchy of premises used by those brewers. The larger businesses remained on the same site for generations and the small businesses set up, and left, new sites. This suggests both the effects of family settlements but more importantly that the investment in equipment was increasingly too substantial for it to be moved economically. This is another indicator of how the industry had developed.

Four premises used for brewing over several generations can be identified. 18, Court Street; 15-17, Preston Street (now The Alexander Centre); part of 2-6, Preston Street; and 24, West Street.

The location of the William Castlocke brewery is debatable. It has been suggested that he ran the abbey brew house as a commercial operation using existing personnel and/or he took it over at the Dissolution and founded his brewery from there. This is unlikely. There was specific objection to such action within the order and William was described as a beer exporter in 1525, years before the dissolution of the abbey. There is no clear evidence of what happened to the abbey brew house after the Dissolution of the Abbey in 1536. If the brew house were being used by William the thorough surveys of the royal commissioners and subsequent grants would have noted that. They do not. An indenture of 1536[93] refers to the lease of the brew house and, inter alia, of 7 gallons of servants ale and the dregs from the brews to Stephen Motte of Davington for 20 years. In 1544 the brew house was still standing.[94] By 1550 the brew house and garden attached was let to William's son John Castlocke. According to Telfer the Abbey brew house was converted to a cottage.[95] The lease may signify nothing about the origins of the brewery and it may have misled historians for generations.

By 1541 William is described as a brewer so he had a brew house somewhere.[96] The list of his property outside the abbey precinct, in Abbey Street, Market Place and Church Street, in 1532, gives no clues to its whereabouts.[97] If it were inside the Abbey demesne, as opposed to the Abbey precinct, it would not appear in the Faversham Manor Rentals. It is possible that it was there, near the Standard Quay.

Evidence of when the brewery settled at 18 Court Street is also lacking but the occupier at that date is interesting. In 1532 the house was owned, but not necessarily occupied by, Henry Crispe of Quex Park, Birchington. He was a very successful East Kent merchant and farmer in the rich barley belt of the Isle of Thanet. His activities would have been well within those of the Castlockes. Further inconclusive evidence connects the two. When the northern block of 18 Court Street was rebuilt in the early nineteenth century some large barge boards emerged. They were carved with shields with fleur de lys, a cross with cherubs and the arms of England with the dragon and greyhound supporters and the initials WC and IC 1544, 35 Henry VIII.[98] Did this refer to William Castlocke and a wife whose initial was J or I or to his son John?

For nearly thirty years there is no evidence for what 18 Court Street was used for, but in 1573 William's grandson John Castlocke II was living there.[99] That his brewing business was then modest suggests that the brewery of his father and grandfather had either run down or ceased.

Thereafter the business grew and this site has ever since, for nearly 450 years, been a brewery from which Shepherd Neame is descended.

Numbers 15 to 17 Preston Street can claim to be the oldest identified brewing site in Faversham and one that may have been used as such for 200 years. In 1463 the premises were transferred from John Roger, William Barbour (a brewer) and Nicholas Wyndout to John Orwell, (a brewer).[100] In 1474 they were transferred by John Orwell the elder to 'Willelmo Thornton de Faversham, brewer.'[101] By 1570 they were occupied by Thomas Cole, who died in 1593.[102] In his will[103] Thomas Cole, who had married Barbara Stransham in 1574,[104] states that he had lately purchased his brew house in Preston Street from Robert Stransham, his brother in law. This suggests that the Stranshams had succeeded Barbour, Orwell and Thornton in the business. Coles daughters sold it to his successor brewer William Tomlyn, who remained there until the 1620s.[105]

Further north in Preston Street, between numbers 2 and 6, was another brew house used by a succession of brewers from the 1540s until the early seventeenth century.[106]

The minor brewers were scattered. William Hilton brewed at 24 West Street. Cornelius Dowman and Robert Shrubsole were in Abbey Street and Court Street and the other brewers appear at various locations for short periods.[107]

In addition to the details of succession and premises the relative importance of the brewers of the sixteenth century is supported by the size of their operations. This is defined by the numbers of their servants as set out in the Faversham Muster Assessments from 1570 to 1600.[108] A servant in this context meant a male business employee rather than a domestic servant.

Thomas Cole emerges as the largest brewer. In 1570 he had four servants; James Wylye, William East, Robert Rogers and John Edgar. In 1573 he had six servants, who included William Tomlin, his successor in the business. From 1583 to 1591 he had seven servants. Not only does this show a substantial operation but suggests that Cole had not set up a new business as a young man,[109] but taken over a large existing business.

At the same time the Stranshams had a smaller business. George, who died in 1576,[110] had four servants. Richard who died in 1583[111] had three in 1583.

John Castlocke II had a smaller business which he appears to have been building up. In 1573 he had one servant, Fowler Derelove. In 1574 he had two servants; Harry Myller and Anthony Brage. In 1580 he had two servants; Fowler Derelove and Thomas Northe. In 1583 he had Thomas Northe and John Conynge as servants. In 1584 he had his son, John Castlocke III junior, and John Couggan as servants. In 1591 there were three servants; Henry Waterman, Henry Adye and

John Danyell. In 1600 there were five; John Castlocke III junior, Henry Adye, John Dannyell, Anstyd and Davye Bowen.

The lesser brewers had fewer servants. William and Robert Hilton had one in 1600, Bartholemew Younge, and possibly George Dix earlier. Clement Oldfield had one in 1574. Richard Huttchyne had one servant, Richard Pyersse in 1583 and a second, John Brooke, in 1584 to 1590. Cornelius Dowman had no servants. Robert Shrubsole had no servants. William Wilson was a brewer but a servant of Richard Tillman, a grain merchant, in the 1580s. Michael Perryie had no servants in the 1580s.

One other type of semi-professional brewer needs to be mentioned, the victualler brewer or inn keeper/tavern keeper, who brewed beer on his premises. By 1700 50% of beer for sale in England was supposed to have been produced by common brewers and 50% by brewing victuallers.[112] 150 years earlier in Faversham the evidence suggests the opposite. Whilst the data here is slender, neither of the two Faversham victuallers, whose Probate Inventories survive for the late sixteenth century,[113] had brewing equipment recorded. John Skyre of the Fleur de Lys, 15 Market Place, who died in 1577, and Thomas Bealkes, both inn holder and Jurat, who died in 1582, were both senior townsmen most likely to have brewing equipment if victualler brewers were common in the late sixteenth century.

Despite the presence of the common brewer in sixteenth century Faversham, domestic brewing continued to be a local source for the supply of beer and ale. As with the brewers, there was a hierarchy of production here, from townsmen with a dedicated room down to householders with a tub in the kitchen. Just how prevalent home brewing was is very difficult to calculate as Probate Inventories are the sole source of information.[114] In the 122 Probate Inventories which are listed between 1565 and 1587 brewing is mentioned in only 8. In other words, 93% of recorded households, which included most of the leading townsmen, such as Thomas Mustard the grocer and benefactor of Faversham, had no recorded brewing equipment.

A very few of the larger premises had a brew house, separated from the main house, like some kitchens, to avoid fire. These were owned by major townsmen. One such is recorded in 1572 as owned by Edward Blackwell Esq. A little further down the social scale seven references survive to townsmen with brewing equipment in the kitchen. In 1570 William Saker, a yeoman at Abbey Farm, in 1585 William Taylor, a yeoman, in 1570 Edward Russell, a tanner, in 1578 Leonard Fidge, a tanner and farmer, and in 1585 Dennys Greenstreet, a widow, all had brewing equipment in their kitchens. In 1579 Robert Chapman had brewing equipment in his botting house and in 1579 John Wreake, a Jurat of Faversham, had brewing equipment in his cellar.

A similar pattern, based on equally slender statistical evidence, emerges for the villages. In Graveney in 1579 Stephen Napleton, a farmer and blacksmith, had a brew house; and in Ospringe in 1578 John Greenstreet, a farmer, had brewing equipment in his kitchen. Conversely, in 1574 Thomas Drayton a Preston yeoman, in 1574 Thomas Harryngton a Preston gentleman and in 1586 Peter Greenstreet in Ospringe, had no brewing equipment listed at their deaths.

How far rudimentary brewing was carried out further down the social scale is unknown. Many townsmen had the means to buy their brew but for the poorer townsmen it may have been cheaper for them to produce a variable 'noxious brew', of a little malt added to hot water with a few herbs or hops to flavour. That at least kept them alive. At the bottom of society, at the end of the century, the poor were dependent upon charity from the Poor Law guardians, paid for by the townsmen, and on weak beer probably brewed by the common brewers.

The sophistication of the brewing equipment is another indicator of the relative importance of the producer. Once again data is sparse but shows the relative size and values of operations.[115]

The Abbey brew house, which had to be efficient and in good repair right up to the Dissolution, is an example of what a common brewer would have had. In 1535 it is described as:[116]

Item
A greate ketill of cooper price £6. 13. 4.
A greate brasse ketill price £0. 13. 4.
A cestern of lede with other ledes waying XX hundred price the pound ob., £4. 3. 4.
A messhing ton and 4 yeldyng tonnes price £2. 0. 0.
A brokyn coper weyng two hundred pounds total £1. 5. 0.
2 last of old kynderkyns price £0. 6. 0.
4 kelers and 2 ryndges price £0. 3. 6.
A clensyng cyve price 6d.
4 taberdes of ledd waying a hundrith pound price £0. 4. 2.
Total £15. 9. 6.

That is about £30 at 1580 values.

No descriptions of the brew houses of the Faversham common brewers have survived before the 1660s.What they actually looked like can be assumed from the remarkable surviving late Elizabethan brew house at Lacock Abbey in Wiltshire.

Further down the scale a number of descriptions have survived.[117] In 1579 Stephen Napleton, farmer and blacksmith at Graveney, had:

In the Brew House
A yealinge tonne
A colesate
A Oestorn

A Brwinge Tonne
With other smale tubbes
Total £3. 6. 4.

In the Drincke House
14 barrells and other vessels £1.1.0.
4 bottels £0. 5. 0.

In 1570 William Saker, yeoman at Abbey Farm Faversham had:

In the Kyttchyn
All the brewinge vessells, tubb & Kylderkyns £2. 0. 0.

In 1570 Edward Russell, tanner, had:

In the Kytchen
A furnes, a brewinge tubb, an elinge tonne with other tubbes £1. 6. 8.

Fidge in 1578 had brewing equipment in his kitchen valued at £1 and John Wreake had brewing equipment in his cellar valued at £1.4.0.

The capacity for production, based upon these values, clearly varied greatly from the commercial brewer to the home brewer. A brew house like that of the Abbey was worth twenty times that of a prosperous yeoman like William Saker.

The fourth source of ale and beer was from imports through the port of Faversham. The volumes were highly variable during the century and they have as much to say about the development of the brewing industry in Faversham and drinking tastes as the sources of supply. The remarkable survival of the Sandwich and Faversham Port Books or Customs records shows this development with some accuracy.[118]

Up to at least 1544 Faversham was importing beer from Flanders (modern Belgium). In the six months between October 1543 and March 1544, for which detailed records survive, the port received 12 barrels, 63 tuns and 27 pipes of beer. The values were £12, £63 and £13. 10. 0. respectively or £88. 10. 0. in total. There were 21 shipments from Ostend, 6 from Flushing, 2 from Neweport and 1 each from Rotterdam and Bryle. These shipments were all by Flemmings and not by Faversham men. When these quantities are converted into gallons and then matched with annual individual consumption their modest significance becomes obvious.

By the 1570s the balance of oversees trade in beer had reversed and by the 1580s Faversham was becoming a very modest exporter. In 1576/7, 1587/8, 1590/1, 1594/5 and 1598, the years for which overseas imports are recorded, no beer was imported from abroad to Faversham. In 1587/1588 7 small cargoes of beer, comprising 8 pipes and 7 tuns, were exported from Faversham. These went to Camphier, Flushing, Quinbowwe and Midleborough. Faversham's coastal trade with London, both inwards and outwards, which was substantial for a range of agricultural produce, records no shipments of beer. These figures suggest that Faversham was self sufficient in beer production by the third quarter of the sixteenth century.

No production figures of Faversham brewers survive before the late eighteenth century, but given the details of the sector tentative estimates of the ranges of barrelage outputs can be made. These can only give an idea of what these early brewers may have produced. This exercise is a model through which to attempt to envisage how big or small the sixteenth century Faversham brewers were.

Take the demand side first. The population of Faversham in 1575 was about 1500 of whom possibly half were adults and half were children. If they drank a gallon of beer or ale and half a gallon of beer or ale a day respectively, annual consumption would have been 410,000 gallons or 11,400 (modern 36 gallon barrels) barrels per year. To that local demand has to be added the demand of visiting travellers and seamen. If the town had 40 of these per day drinking one gallon each the additional demand would be 15,000 gallons or 410 barrels. This gives a total demand of nearly 12,000 barrels per year. To this has to be added beer or ale required by the villages and by the coastal trade to London. As brewing in the countryside was widespread and as virtually no beer or ale was sent out by sea,[119] or known to have been sent out by road, these amounts were probabaly insignificant.

Now take the supply side. Import of beer to Faversham by sea was negligible[120] and unless there were an as yet undiscovered quality brewer outside the town that source of supply was also negligible. The supply therefore depended upon town producers; common brewers, victualler brewers and private houses. From the evidence for late sixteenth century Faversham, based on the Probate Inventories, victualler brewing was unknown and home brewing was carried out by only 7% of the more prosperous townsmen. For this exercise 50% of brewing output is taken as supplied by the brewers. This figure may be too low.

From this the output of the Faversham brewers can be postulated. Taking the numbers of brewers whose relative sizes are verified by details of their premises and succession data, plus the numbers of their servants as the basis of the size and hence production of each brewer, a tentative estimate of output can be made.

In 1575 there were 17 brewers and servants. Thomas Cole plus 7 men accounted therefore for 41% of production; George Stransham plus 5 men for 29%; John Castlocke II plus 3 men for 18%; Cornelius Dowman plus 1 man and Richard Stransham plus 1 man accounted for 6% each. The total production of the Faversham common brewers is taken as 50 % of 12,000 barrels, being

6,000 barrels per annum. Today, John Castlocke's successor, Shepherd Neame, produces 6,000 barrels per week.

Using these figures, Thomas Cole was brewing 2460 barrels per annum or 47 barrels per week; George Stransham was brewing 1740 barrels per annum or 33 barrels per week; John Castlocke II was brewing 1080 barrels per annum or 21 barrels per week; and Cornelius Dowman and Richard Stransham were brewing 360 barrels each per annum or 7 barrels per week. On the evidence available it is reasonable to assume this was beer not ale.

In 1500 hopped ale or beer was still a novelty but by 1560 it was widespread as the common drink. The change in product was a top down process rather than a bottom up process.

The use of the name beer brewer in Faversham is indicative of this change. Laurence Stransham, the early common brewer, was referred to as a brewer in 1511. William Castlocke was exporting beer in 1525 but in 1540 he was referred to as a brewer not a beer brewer. Only in 1550 was John Castlocke I, his son, referred to as a beer brewer. This implies a distinction at that time. In the 1550s and 1560s Thomas Tenacre and William Maycott were brewers but their premises are referred to as a beer house which suggests they were beer brewers. John Perte who died in 1571, Michael Join who died in 1593 and Cornelius Dowman, all small producers, were each called beer brewer. George Stransham, who died in 1576, and Thomas Cole who died in 1593, were leading brewers but were referred to only as brewer. Possibly by then the terms were inter changeable. By the late sixteenth century all the big producers were called beer brewers; John Castlocke II, Richard Stransham and William Tomlyn.

What is interesting is that the Castlocke family were all described as beer brewers from the 1540s which suggests they were the leading promoters of the new product beer. The three small producers, Perte, Join and Dowman, may also have been early specialists promoting the new product. The description of others as brewers may have been the use of a generic term or implied they still produced ale as well as beer and did not fully embrace the new product.

To understand the spread of beer consumption some indicators are given by the probate inventories. In 1568 William Bennet,[121] an innholder, had four barrels of beer valued at 26/8 in his cellar and owed £10 for beer to George Stransham and £7 for beer to Thomas Oldfield. Taking the average price above of 6/10 per barrel that means he owed them for about 50 barrels of beer. No ale is recorded on his premises. This shows that at least at the upper end of the victuallers market the drinking of beer was common.

Evidence from private houses is mixed. No beer or ale is recorded but malt is recorded in several houses. Henry Philpott in 1570 had two malting tuns and a malt loft. William Saker had a malt querne in his kitchen in 1570. Thomas Mustard, the grocer, in 1575 had 'a hundred of hoppes' valued at 8/- in his storehouse. Leonard Fidge had eight quarters of malt and barley in 1578. In the same year John Wreake, jurat, had twelve bushels of malt valued at 16/-.

Beer was clearly supplanting ale as the staple drink by the mid sixteenth century, but the speed at which that was happening is difficult to quantify. The reference to payments by the Corporation of Faversham for alcohol in the Town Books is a guide, as this is a consistent source for a range of activities. In 1520 wine, beer and ale were given to the King and Queen at Faversham.[122] In 1557 and later in 1563 beer, but not ale, and wine were given the Lord Warden of the Cinque Ports.[123] For the annual Lammas night watch beer and not ale was given from at least 1563.[124] One significant sign of how far down the social scale beer had penetrated was the giving of beer, not ale, to the labourers constructing the Guildhall in 1575 and to the labourers digging gravel from the gravel pits in 1577.[125] Ale as a commodity disappears from the Town Books from the 1520s which suggests that beer was much more common at a much earlier date than previously thought.

Turning now from the sources of production to the ingredients of beer and ale, of hops, malt and water, changes in the sector in the sixteenth century are also evident. Whilst malt was produced locally for ale, hops were at first imported but by the end of the century the demand for them was being fulfilled by the home grown. The demand for a new product gradually spawned a new agricultural specialism.

At the same time that beer was being imported to Faversham from the Low Countries so were hops, often in the same shipments. The earliest reference to the import of hops to Faversham is in 1533. Henry Hatch,[126] the merchant and benefactor of Faversham, imported 600lbs of hops on the ship of Christopher Vanster. Ten years later the cargoes were brought in by twelve merchants, all of whom were beer importers to Faversham. Between October 1543 and March 1544, the first period for which lists of figures are available,[127] there were 23 shipments of hops into Faversham. These consisted of 73 pockets, 3 half pockets and 2 quarter pockets of hops. As each pocket weighed between 2 1/2cwt and 1 1/2cwt at that date[128] that was an average total of 150cwt of hops for one season. These were substantial figures that by the size cannot have been achieved in a single year, but must have been achieved after some years of trading. This was the result of the growing demand for beer.

If this were the quantity of the raw material available what volume of beer did this produce at the breweries? For this date no figures are known, but by the 1830s one hundredweight of hops produced 25 barrels of beer.[129] Using the same ratios for the earlier period, 150cwt of hops would have produced 3750 barrels of beer. This estimated figure of production for 1544 is not inconsistent with the growth of production of 6,000 barrels of beer thirty years later in 1575. This does not of course take account of any hops that may have came to Faversham by road.

By 1576/7 the sourcing of hops had changed. The imports from the Low Countries had dropped to a mere 12 pockets or 24cwt. With the exception of one pocket from Cornelio Dolphman, the remainder were brought in by Faversham merchants in Faversham vessels. Nicholas Adye imported 2 pockets; John Tyndall imported 3 pockets; and John Lawrence 6 pockets.[130] In 1590/1 only 2 pockets of hops were imported from the Low Countries;[131] in 1594/5 only 4 pockets were imported;[132] and in 1598 only 3 pockets were imported.[133] The inference that Faversham was becoming self sufficient in local hops seems proven by the outwards coastal trade with London from September 1598 to September 1599. In that year four Faversham merchants, John Lawrence, Thomas Henman, John Boney and Thomas Tassell consigned 73 pockets of hops to the London market. In 30 years Faversham had changed from being a net purchaser of hops from Europe to being a net seller of home grown hops to London.

If Faversham were able to produce such a surplus, albeit in a year probably with an exceptional crop, where were the hops grown and how many acres were planted? If Faversham were brewing 6,000 barrels of beer per annum that would have required 240cwt of hops. That would have required cultivation of about 38 acres, based again on the ratios of the 1830s.[134] Research to date[135] has suggested that hop growing developed in the Weald of Kent and only later spread to the Faversham and Canterbury areas. As only one local hop garden has been conclusively identified in Faversham this early, at Homestall Farm by 1590,[136] and the term hop grower first used in the early eighteenth century, some credence might be given to this theory. However, as transport from the Weald was notoriously bad and expensive, especially in the autumn when the hops were picked, it is difficult to believe this was the unrecorded source of supply by road. There must have been hop gardens around Faversham and in the villages but because they were a few acres at most they were only an incidental part of the farmers production and hence went unrecorded.

The origin of the malt used for both ale and beer brewing in Faversham is easier to follow. Much barley was grown locally and the production of malt was widespread in the town. This production was not only sufficient for brewing purposes but produced substantial surpluses for export.

As malt was the basis of the production of ale it is not surprising that the town had developed a malt industry. Barley grew well on the farms south of Faversham, and whilst not of the quality of that grown in the Isle of Thanet, it was of a reasonable standard. It could be brought into the town by road for malting or brought in ready malted at low cost. There are no references to it being imported by sea into Faversham.[137] In the 1570s and 1580s the town probably had limited surpluses, or was not yet reacting to the demand of London, as no shipments to London or abroad are recorded. From the 1590s that situation reversed. In 1598/9 alone, Faversham sent up to London 201 separate cargoes of malt, averaging 20 bushels each. 4000 quarters were substantial quantities.[138]

The malt trade was spread but there were a few important merchants or 'partnerships'. At the top was Alexander Ore who made 20 shipments; next came Jacob Worceter who made 11 shipments and Anthony Bodle, either by himself or with others, made 11 shipments; then came Richard Tilman with 8 shipments. Thereafter dozens of small merchants made one or two shipments.

Amongst the names of the maltsters are both John Castlocke II and Robert Stransham. This suggests that these brewers were malting for their own needs and shipping surpluses up to London. Castlocke sent up 7 cargoes totalling 260 quarters and Stransham sent up 2 cargoes of 55 quarters of malt.

The conversion of the quantities of malt sent to London into barrels of beer produced from them helps to put the malt trade into perspective. For this exercise, strong beer is taken as equivalent to Shepherd Neame's Spitfire, (ALC 4.2% VOL.) so 1 quarter of malt would have produced 6 barrels of beer.[139] 4000 quarters of malt would have produced 24,000 barrels of beer.That in turn would have been sufficient for 3000 people, or double the population of Faversham at that period.

The third ingredient of beer is water. The quality and availability of it in the sixteenth century was as significant as it is today and it can be no accident that the two Faversham breweries which survived all the others, by the nineteenth century, were located where they were.

The hydrogeology of the Castlocke site predisposed this brewery to out-perform ultimately the others. The brewery well was, and still is, a natural spring of water whose aquifer is the chalk, covered by a thin layer of clay. Pure water bubbles naturally to the surface, as it did until about 1900 in Conduit Street, at the rear of the Brewery, where the water conduit or well of the town was sited. At the other old brewery sites of the Stranshams and Cole in Preston Street it did not. Their wells, albeit not very deep, had to be sunk and maintained and that added to costs.

The costs of agricultural products fluctuated from season to season but the price of beer was regulated by the Town Corporation. As the leading brewers were all townsmen collectively they could at least set a reasonable price each year. What the market place could do was to 'regulate' by purchase demand the variety in quality of a product coming from so many sources.

For the price of beer the Faversham Town Books provide a consistent source, over a long period. Beer came in two strengths, strong beer and small beer, and was priced accordingly. In 1575 and 1578 a kilderkin of strong beer cost 3/6d. In 1572 and 1573 a kilderkin of (presumably) small beer cost 2/3d. In 1576 two kilderkins of 'towne beare' cost 4/4d.[140 141]

Such is the varied background to the production of beer, but the distribution of the product was equally varied and fluctuated over time to take advantage of opportunities as they arose. There were four distribution channels. There were sales to private households, sales through taverns and inns, sales to London and coastal ports and miscellaneous sales.

The first channel of sales was direct private trade. The more prosperous families and tradesmen probably bought direct from the brewers. They drank enough to take 2 kilderkins or a barrel (30 gallons in sixteenth century England) a week, which would have kept long enough before going sour. A sample household of two adults, two children and a servant probably drank 4 gallons of beer a day which is 28 gallons per week. That would make a weekly delivery viable. Small families and the poor probably had neither adequate demand, nor the money, to make it viable for them to take even a kilderkin a week. They could have collected a pot of beer as needed from the brewers, the tippling houses or from a neighbour, but there is no evidence one way or the other.[142] Private trade to private households was still substantial for Faversham brewers in the mid nineteenth century.

The second, and much better documented, channel of sales was through the inns, taverns, tippling houses and ale houses. There was a wide range of outlets for which the names of owners, occupiers and guarantors have survived in part from the 1530s. This gives an insight into the structure of the public house trade at an early date and early suggestions of tied houses.

By 1532 at least twelve 'public houses' can be identified.[143] The leading six were sited centrally round the Market Place. The Ship and the Fleur de Lys were at numbers 16 and 15; the Bear, the Garrett and the Horn were at numbers 1-3 and 6. Further out in Preston Street was the Saracens Head and on the opposite side of the road were the George and the Swan. At 25 Court Street was the Anchor and nearby was the Cock. To the west were the Greyhound at 6-8 West Street and opposite at 116 West Street was the Crowne. Of these the Bear was mentioned as early as 1488 in the will of Richard Thornbury.[144] Others existed but cannot be located with certainty. [Table 5]

By the 1570s more names appear. In Preston Street were the Maypole, the Sheeres, the Red Lion and the Squire. Elsewhere were the White Horse and the Keys. The numbers of 'public houses' was never static, especially at the lower end. Between 1570 and 1594[145] the numbers of houses granted annual licenses, or Recognisances, by the Corporation fluctuated between 17 in 1570, 15 in 1577, 24 in 1591 and to 20 in 1594. In 1577 the national Return of Inns Taverns and Alehouses notes 13 alehouses and 2 inns for Faversham Town plus 20 alehouses scattered throughout the Hundred of Faversham.[146] These figures suggest at least a modest growth in the numbers of sales outlets but at the same time some houses ceased to be public houses and others appeared in their place.

Ownership of these houses was distinct from occupation. Most owners were content to receive rents rather than to take trading risks. The owners of the 11 major houses were senior Faversham townsmen. John Upton, for example, who owned the Anker was a mayor. Richard Wood, who died in 1570, owned the Crowne, the George and the Kings Head.[147] Henry Hatch, the great Faversham merchant and benefactor had owned the Queens Arms in Market Place and the Rose in Preston Street in the 1530s.[148] Edward Harris, who owned the Horn, was a Jurat in 1587.[149]

A few owners had connections with the brewing industry. Robert Withiot, the reforming mayor of Faversham, who died in 1511, owned the Crowne in West Street.[150] He owned the Brewhouse and the Bakehouse in Partridge Lane as well as a malthouse and his great house, 1-4 East Street, in 1507. The Horne in Market Place was owned by Alexander Oers, before 1604,[151] In 1598 he was the biggest exporter of malt from Faversham.[152] In his will of 1586 Edward Harris wished the Horne to be sold by Thomas Cole, the Preston Street brewer.[153] It was bought by the maltster with whom he probably traded.

The only brewing family recorded as owning a public house was the Stransham family. In the late sixteenth century they owned the Bear at Market Place.[154] One beer brewer, Cornelius Dowman, is recorded as a tippler, or publican, in 1570,[155] but not in later lists. The brewing sector had a long way to go before tied houses were the norm.

Very occasionally owners were licensees. Thomas Hawkes owned and occupied the Ship, at 16 Market Place, from at least 1570 until his death in 1589.[156] He clearly had additional, and probably related, business interests as he was described as yeoman in his will. After his death his widow, Luce, bequeathed it to her son Robert Edmondes but by then it was tenanted by John Wattes.[157] The other example is John Skyre. By 1577, when he died, he was both owner and occupier of the Fleur de Lys, at 15 Market Place.[158] The Ship was clearly the more substantial of the two; in 1584 Hawkes had three servants. These two houses were exceptional assets, in as much as they were in the commercial centre of the town with good rear access. The licensees were the only ones described as innholders and not tippling house keepers.

What is also evident is the constant change in ownership of these premises. Licensed houses did not remain with a family over several generations. This is shown by the comparison of the bequests in wills of the 1580s and 1590s with the ownership lists of 1604 and 1608.[159] In 1524 the Saracens Head was bequeathed by Alice Barbour, the widow of John, to William Wyer.[160] By

1532 it was out of their ownership. By the 1580s it was owned by the Crofts and in 1591 Alverye Croft bequeathed it to her son Thomas.[161] By 1604 it was no longer a licensed house. The early example of the Ship is given above and by 1604 it was owned by William Finch. The ownership of the Fleur de Lys was similar; from John Skyre in the 1570s, it had passed to Edward Murfield by 1604.

The occupiers, or licensees, of the houses were equally transient men, or women.[162] In 1570 licenses were issued to 15 men. By 1577 only two of those licensees, Robert Rye and John Hawsnothe, still held licenses. In 1577 licenses were issued to 17 people. By 1590 only Robert Rye still held one. In 1590 licenses were issued to 17 men. By 1601 there were 19 licensees, of whom two were women, but only 3, or 15%, had held licensees 9 years before.

Not only were the licensees transient but very few were prominent townsmen. None were mayors or jurats and only three were commoners. They were all lesser men than the owners. Only one, for example, was able to sign his name. Moreover, many were only part time licensees. In 1570 of the 15 licensees 6, or 40%, had other occupations. There was a cooper, a taylor, a bricklayer, a sheerman, a waterman and Dowman the beer brewer. By 1601 the situation had changed further. There were 2 innkeepers, 1 brewer and 16 licensees, or 75%, with other occupations. This suggests that either returns were insufficient to support many or that tippling provided a useful additional income for many tradesmen or that some houses were managed by the unnamed.

Such turnovers beg interesting questions about the economy of a town like Faversham at that date. Was there a widespread failure of heirs? Were there more remunerative investment opportunities elsewhere? Whatever the answer is, the impression is of a very fluid market place if not an endemic 'short-termism'.

For the history of Faversham's 'tied houses' these Recognisances are revealing. Every licensee named two guarantors, of £5 each, for his good behaviour and against these names are occupations. Brewers, maltsters and bakers gradually predominate.

In 1570 no brewers or maltsters provided guarantees. In 1577 and 1580 John Castlocke, beer brewer, provided guarantees for 2 tippling house keepers and Richard Stransham, beer brewer provided 1. In 1589 Richard Huttchyne and Michael Perryie, beer brewers, each provided 1 guarantee. In 1590 William Hilton provided 1 guarantee whilst William Tomlin provided 4 guarantees to 17 houses. In 1591 Hilton provided 6 guarantees and Tomlin 6 guarantees to 24 houses. In 1601 Tomlin provided 5 guarantees, Robert Hilton provided 3, John Castlocke gent. provided 2 and Jacob Worncester the maltster provided 4 guarantees for 19 houses. In 1590 and 1601 the remaining guarantors were predominantly bakers, especially George Cruttall. [Table 6]

In 1577 only 20% of the houses were guaranteed by brewers. By 1591 50% of the houses were guaranteed by brewers. In 1601 55% of the houses were guaranteed by brewers and 25% by a maltster. Within 25 years a new pattern of operation had emerged. This novel idea may have been introduced by John Castlocke, who was a young man having to break into an existing market but, soon after the idea was extended by his brewer competitors, William Tomlin and Robert Hilton. It was not long for the other big suppliers of houses, the bakers, to follow suit.

What this pattern suggests is at the least a close business association between brewers and maltsters and at the most a one step remove from a tied house. The question is why in the sixteenth century, when failure of one unregulated business meant immediate danger to another, would anyone give a guarantee. There must have been mutual opportunities to trade profitably and more especially the chance of one to influence or oversee closely the operations of the other by being a preferred supplier. The brewers supplied the beer, the maltsters supplied the malt to the brewers, and possibly to victualler brewers, and the bakers supplied bread to the houses for customers to eat with their drink. Each was protecting their market, or trying to expand it, by a novel mechanism.

The third channel of trade of beer was sea-born trade. Whilst there was potential for such trade the data available suggests that either the Faversham beer brewers had not yet reached the critical size for substantial surpluses, above local demand, to be available to trade; or that the demand from elsewhere had not yet outreached its own local brewers. The crops of hops in these early days were so variable that supply could not be guaranteed.

In 1559, 1560 and 1564 three stray references appear in the Town Books to the shipping of beer from Faversham.[163] The destinations are unspecified and repeated neither before nor after. Between 1570 and 1600 sea-born trade in beer from Faversham is recorded in only one year; that is 1587/8[164] and even that may have had something to do with provisioning our allies in the Low Countries. Beer totalling 8 pipes and 7 tons was shipped in 7 trips to Camphier, Flushing, Quinbowwe and Middleborough. This was sent to Flanders, the present day Belgium, but nothing was sent to London, the main destination of the towns coastal trade. Undisclosed trade in beer from the Cinque Ports is implied in a note of the Privy Council in 1576/7.[165] 'Their Lordships understand that in sundry creeks under his jurisdiction divers brewing houses have been of late set up from whence secretly great quantities of beer are conveyed...' In the same period there was likewise no outwards trade in hops. Thereafter the figures are different.

The fourth channel of trade for the brewers was miscellaneous; largely Corporation or national. Municipal events needed beer brewed locally. For example in 1552 Thomas Teneker was paid for beer for Lammas Night.[166] In 1573 'Master Castlocke was paid for one kilderkin of beer for (town business in the Isle of ) Harty'.[167] The foreign adventures of the period also needed provisioning and Faversham as a Cinque Port limb was expected to provide it. This took the form of ingredients, rather than beer the finished product, although in 1591 there is a request from the town to government for payment for victualling the Portugese Voyage.[168] In 1580 the town had to provide hops and in 1600 'there was a great want of malt towards provision of beer for the Navy...and Kent was required to provide 400 Quaters...'[169]

This in outline is the range of outlets through which sales were made and from these at least an estimate of the relative sales volumes can be made. Beer or ale was drunk by everyone throughout the day; at home and at work, which often went on until dusk. Assuming that only a small part of the day, at the end, was available for adult males to drink at ale houses probably as little as 10% of the consumption of inhabitants was there.[170] If visitors to the town swelled numbers by only 5% daily[171] and they drank only at ale houses then only 15% of total beer production would have been drunk there. If the assumption that 50% of brewing was home brewing holds then 30% of brewers production was sold to ale houses and 70% to private houses. These are but estimates but the aim is to illustrate how the brewing trade probably operated in the sixteenth century and what were the volumes.

In addition to brewing, some in the sector had other commercial interests. William Castlocke was a merchant as well as a brewer early in the century. In 1598 and 1599 John Castlocke was sending quantities of malt and triticis[172] to London. He had various partnerships for these cargoes with John Cook, William Hayman or Joseph Bestpitche.[173] In 1586 he had a 21 years lease of the towns Little Storehouse. Three years later he is recorded as assigning his lease on the Middle Storehouse.[174] By 1604 he owned a portfolio of property that was leased out. He owned several houses, orchards and a malthouse in Court Street east and land and orchards in West Street and Kingsfield in Preston Street.[175] The Stranshams certainly had farming interests at Ospringe.

Unlike many merchants in sixteenth century Faversham who were general merchants, the brewers appear to have followed one trade with only minor other interests or, in relation to property, as investors of surplus capital. Brewing appears to have created a specialism earlier than many other industries. The widespread lack of specialism at this date probably explains why so many prosperous townsmen showed no occupation in their wills.

Further down the scale the publicans certainly had other occupations, as outlined above. In 1570 only 40% had other occupations. By 1601 75% had other occupations.

In addition to their commercial lives the more prosperous merchants continued to take an active part in town affairs. Participation in the affairs of the Town Corporation gave a number of benefits beyond mere reflection of commercial success or ambition or status in a small community. It gave access to modest patronage and the power of 'policing' through the small courts, at a time when there was no local bureaucracy nor local services. Most importantly it gave access to a club where networking led to commercial opportunities.

All the brewers followed similar routes into and through civic life. They had to become freemen in order to practice their trade. From there they became commoners, or common council men, then jurats, or aldermen, and then many became mayor. At the same time they fulfilled a number of administrative and quasi-judicial functions. Later in the century some executed government orders sent to the Corporation through the Lords Lieutenant or direct from the Council in London. Personal expenditure was usually the price they had to pay.

William Castlocke was a commoner by 1516 and a jurat in 1532. Despite the importance of his brother, John the Abbot, he never became mayor. In 1542 he contributed 5 marks to the Kings Loan and in 1549 he and his son John Castlocke I contributed 40/- and 20/- respectively to a Benevolence from the Cinque Ports to the crown.[176] John Castlocke I was a commoner by 1543, a chamberlain, or collector of the revenues of the town, in 1546/7, a churchwarden in 1551 and a jurat by 1554.[177]

His son, John Castlocke II, was a jurat by 1574 and mayor of Faversham in 1588. At the time of war in Europe with Spain, he was deeply involved in the organisation of defence. In 1588 he raised the Cess, or tax upon the householders of the town, to pay for the ship T.S.Hazard as part of the contribution of the Cinque Ports to the fleet. In 1592 he personally paid £30 for buttling and victualling of soldiers for the voyage to Portugal. In 1596 he negotiated with Dover, the head Cinque Port, the towns 25% contribution towards furnishing for 5 months a 160 tons vessel with victuals, mariners and munitions. The Cess raised was £300. In Faversham he was a Captain of the Trained Bands, a home defence militia, in 1591 and 1596. At the same time he was representing Faversham at Cinque Ports meetings, in Kent and in London. In 1597 he represented, with others, Faversham at the Court of the Guestling at Rye, in 1598 he attended the High Court of Shepway at Bekesbourne and in 1600 at London.[178] At the same time he was sitting as a 'justice' at the towns Court of Portmote.[179]

The Stransham family was equally prominent in town governance. Laurence Stransham was mayor in 1511. His descendants were commoners and jurats until they withdrew from town affairs at the end of the century. For some years two or three Stranshams were members of the town council. By 1567 Thomas and George were both jurats.

Other families were similar. Robert Withiott was mayor in 1506/7 and 1509/10. John Finch was mayor in 1573 and Thomas Cole was three times mayor, in 1575, 1582 and 1591. His successor William Tomlyn followed suit later.[180]

Further down the scale the hierarchy of the lesser brewers is reflected in the hierarchy of their civic lives. They would all have to have been freemen. Thomas Tenaker was a commoner by 1547 but never a jurat. William Maycott was a freeman in 1543 and a jurat in 1551. Other brewers like Dowman never became jurats. None of these men became mayors.

None of the licensees got even that far. None became commoners nor jurats and none became mayor. This is another example of the economic and social hierarchy of the brewing sector.

The brewers were part of the very broadly based Faversham economy. Faversham was a market town and an industrial town sited on the main London to Dover Road and serving an agricultural hinterland. There were grain merchants, maltsters, brewers, leather workers, metal workers, copperas entrepreneurs and from the 1570s a small gunpowder industry. It was a fishing town and a port close to London. The oyster fishery and fishing industry, which supported many families, was important for the economy as it was counter seasonal. There was a thriving shipping sector. Faversham had also a defined political identity. It was an ancient borough, with charters going back to at least the thirteenth century, and membership of the Cinque Ports, as a limb of Dover. This absorbed the entire commercial elite of the town.

Whilst this is not the place to quantify this economy, it does help to put the brewing sector into perspective. The relative significance of the brewers can be shown by comparing the numbers of servants they employed with those employed by other men.[181] In 1573 at the top end of the scale of the largest employers, defined as those who employed 3 or more men, there were 13 such townsmen who employed 51 'servants' in total. Of those 13 townsmen 2 were brewers, who employed 6 men and 4 men respectively. Only William Saker, a yeoman at Abbey Farm, employed 6 men and only one man, William Cumber, a shoemaker, employed 5. To employ more men than any other business was significant but the numbers of men brewers employed were in absolute terms tiny. Even in the early nineteenth century, by which time the population of Faversham had doubled, Shepherds Brewery with an output of 5000 barrels a year only employed 10 men.[182] It is also important to remember that all of these men were sole proprietors of their businesses and that virtually every house was occupied by a sole proprietor of a business; unlike today when most households are employed by a company. That in itself demonstrates how diffused and fragmented the economy of the town was in the sixteenth century.

The lives of these brewers were however as fragile as the economy of their town was diffused. At their deaths, when the final tally of worldly success or failure was drawn, their ultimate successes appear modest.[183] That should not be so surprising. Demand for beer was static and restricted to a very small area. Moreover, death in middle age made all the difference from death in old age. Each of the brewers owned a house, which incorporated their plant, occasionally some investment property but little money. Thomas Cole, the major brewer of the century died in 1593, probably aged about 48. He bequeathed £295 in cash, mostly made up of a £40 dowry to each of his daughters, and the residue of his personal estate to his wife to bring up the children. In addition to his house and brewery in Preston Street, he bequeathed a property near the Quays and a house and land called Masters in Stone Parish.[184] Richard Hutchin, a smaller sized brewer, died in 1590, probably aged about 35. In his will he bequeathed £110, an annuity of £5 pa., a silver guilt salt sellar, four properties and a few acres in Ospringe.[185] At the other end of the scale the servant brewer William Wilson died in 1592 and left only £3.10.0 plus his house.

One final note of comparison helps to bring Faversham's sixteenth century brewing sector into a wider perspective; that is comparison with the experience of other Kent towns. Canterbury is a good example, not least because it has lists of freemen with their occupations for the period.[186] Faversham has lists of brewers, all of whom would have had to be freemen, drawn from many sources. With a population of about 5000 Canterbury was more than three times the size of Faversham; in other words, Faversham was about 30% of the size of Canterbury. In Canterbury from 1500 to 1525 8 brewers of whom 3 were beer brewers became free. From 1526 to 1550 8 brewers and no named beer brewers became free. From 1551 to 1575 11 brewers of whom 9 were beer brewers became free. From 1576 to 1600 13 brewers of whom 2 were beer brewers became free.

Assuming the Canterbury men brewed throughout the 25 years period in which they became free a direct comparison with Faversham is revealing. In the fifteenth century the numbers of Faversham brewers were 33% of those of Canterbury. From 1500 to 1550 the numbers of Faversham brewers were 40% of those of Canterbury. From 1550 to 1575 the numbers of Faversham brewers were 100% of, or equal to, those of Canterbury. From 1575 to 1600 the numbers of Faversham brewers were 80% of those of Canterbury. These figures suggest that the brewing industry in Faversham became gradually of more significance than that of a major town like Canterbury.

The comparison of the numbers of beer brewers is also interesting. Canterbury had 6 known beer brewers before 1550, whilst Faversham had 1. From 1550 to 1575 Canterbury had 9 beer brewers and Faversham had 4. The growth of beer brewing developed in both towns at the same time but for Faversham the sector appears to have became more important than that in Canterbury.[187]

In summary, by 1600 the brewing industry in Faversham had developed into an important and stable sector. The industry was dominated by a small number of local families, many of whom were able to transfer their businesses at death. These families were leading townsmen who were fully integrated into the wider economic and social fabric of the town. Their channels of distribution were local, in which private trade was the most important and sea-born trade surprisingly small. A number of inns, ale houses and tippling houses had grown up and some of these were guaranteed by, if not actually tied to, leading brewers.

With the popularity of the relatively new hopped beer the greatest sector change was in the product. Ale was displaced as the national drink. From being a foreign imported product, beer became a product made locally but from an imported ingredient, the hop. Soon, hops were grown locally so the end product was made from local produce. A new industry developed.

## CHAPTER FOUR

# Consolidation of the Castlockes: 1600 to 1650

For the fifty years after 1600 the brewing sector in Faversham established in the previous century remained fundamentally unchanged. Production continued to be in the hands of a small number of brewing families and on a limited domestic scale in the homes of townsmen. Of the old brewing families the Castlockes and the Hiltons were the only ones to survive, but even they both failed, for different reasons, by the 1650s. The Castlockes were clearly the leaders who consolidated their social position in the town and maintained their commercial one. However, they were not the only brewers of size.

Distribution continued substantially through private trade and to a growing extent through inns and alehouses, if the growth in their numbers is a guide. Shipment of beer to the burgeoning market of London was very modest, spasmodic and of little significance to the total trade of the brewers. The belief that Faversham's brewing trade grew on the back of the rising London market demand for the finished product of beer is misplaced. What did grow on the back of the London market was the production at and the shipping from Faversham of the raw materials of brewing, hops and malt. The underlying situation was of a product market in Faversham that was saturated, of a local population that was growing very slowly and of a sector that was highly regulated. Lack of growth is not surprising.

The numbers of brewers in any one year fluctuated. Whilst there was a core of long standing larger operators, smaller producers entered the market place and some stayed. [Table 3]. Between 1600 and 1621 the names of 7 brewers in total are known. In 1622 there were 6 brewers which fell to 4 by 1625. In 1638 there were 5 brewers which rose to 7 in 1644 and to 10 in 1649.[188] The Faversham Corporation, which licensed local brewers by issuing a 'fine', stated in 1644 that 'there were more brewers in town than usually there have been'. Succession, the transfer of technology and location varied from business to business.

By comparison to Canterbury for the same period Faversham had become a significant brewing town. Between 1600 and 1625 Canterbury had 12 brewers who were freemen and between 1625 and 1650 Canterbury had 11 brewers who were freemen.[189] Considering that the population of Faversham was only a third of that of Canterbury and that the Faversham brewers were all freemen, the significance becomes obvious. Faversham at that time appears to have been relatively a more significant brewing town than Canterbury.

The leading Faversham brewery for the period remained that of the Castlockes. By 1600 the family had been in Faversham for a century and was the oldest surviving merchant family in the town. John Castlocke II, the third generation, had built up a brewery employing 4 'servants',[190] more than any other brewer. When he died in 1613 he had been sole proprietor for 40 years. The family continued not only because it had a succession of male children over many generations but because from each generation a son came into the business. John Castlocke II assured the succession by taking his eldest son, John Castlocke III, into the business by 1600. This John was another sole proprietor who was in the business for 50 years. About 1625 he in turn took his son, John Castlocke IV, into the business Family continuity was vital to commercial continuity. Only when John Castlocke IV died childless in 1652, and the family became extinct in the male line, did the business pass out of the family. Even then it continued on the same site at 18 Court Street.

A little smaller, but an equally well established brewer, was William Tomlyn, who in 1600 employed 3 servants.[191] He had succeeded Thomas Cole, whose servant he had been since 1573,[192] at 15/17 Preston Street. After his death brewing may have ceased for a time at this site but was taken on later by his son in law, Edward Wright, until 1656.

The other brewing family that survived was that of Hilton. They appeared in Faversham in the early sixteenth century and descendants later developed at least two unconnected breweries. In 1583 William is recorded as brewing at 24 West Street, with 2 servants in 1600. By 1604 this was known as the Flying Horse. His son, Robert, with one servant, continued to brew there until about 1620. At his death in 1624 the property passed to his son, another William, who did not continue brewing but became a Faversham ship owner and master by 1628.[193] The brewery was continued by a 'servant' William Baker[194] until at least 1645[195] and brewing then ceased on the site.

Until 1628 another Hilton, John, was brewing on a scale similar to the Castlockes, probably at a new site, 70/72 Preston Street.[196] Brewing ceased there at his death until John Greenstreet re started a brewery there for a few years in the 1640s. His son Thomas Hilton was probably the brewer who inherited the Castlocke Brewery in 1652.

Yet another Hilton, Richard, as yet not connected to the others, was brewing from about 1630 until his death in 1644,[197] on a scale similar to that of William Baker.[198] At the same time as brewing he was malting and in 1635 was sending both malt and wheat up to London.[199] His location is likewise not yet identified.

Two new breweries of size, similar to the Castlockes, were established in the period. John Scott, set up a new business in Middle Row by 1622 and survived for about 20 years. Francis Windsor took over the Standard Brewhouse in the 1630s but died in 1640. The description of his brewing business is the earliest one that has survived for Faversham.[200] The chance survival of his Probate Inventory gives insight into what a brewery was like at that time. In his house was 'The Customers Office and his Study'. In the 'Wash House' was a load of hop poles valued at 10/-. In 'The Brewhouse' were wagons and horses valued at £45; malt and barley valued at £48; coal valued at £15; 4 1/2 cwt of hops valued at £9; 50 tuns[201] (400 barrels) in hogsheads, barrels and other vessels valued at £20; oasthair and forks valued at £4; brewing movable equipment valued at £1.11.0. The main fixed equipment of copper and tuns is not listed. Little more is known about these men but even in the restricted brewing sector of the seventeenth century there was space for substantial newcomers who survived, albeit for a short time.

One other newcomer needs particular mention. Thomas Baldock is recorded in 1644 as the smallest of the brewers, whose entry was at the lowest possible point. He set up at 88/90 West Street,[202] in one of the poorer streets of Faversham, where he remained for 10 years. Five years later he had become the biggest brewer in Faversham. He appears to have been an entirely self made entrepreneur, with no known relations in Faversham, but with an eye for a chance. That chance was the demise of the Castlocke family and the gap in the market place that created.

The range of market shares of these common brewers was little different from that of the previous century. The Castlockes maintained their share until the end in 1648. They held 25% of the production of the common brewers in Faversham;[203] possibly up a little from the 1590s, when they held 18%. [Table 3]. Throughout the period there were always one or two competitors of the same size. In the 1620s both John Hilton and John Scott had the same 25% market shares when there were only 4 brewers. In 1638 Francis Windsor had 20% of the market share. In 1644 there were 7 brewers competing; John Greenstreete, one of a large Faversham and Ospringe family of farmers, maltsters and merchants,[204] had another 25% share, whilst others held from 18% to the lowest of 4%, held by the new comer, Thomas Baldock. Even in 1649, after the dramatic demise of John Catlocke, his successor William Dix maintained the market share of his old master, albeit that another new comer, Francis Verrier, who lasted only a couple of years, had the same 25% share.

That was the hierarchy of the common brewers but these were not the only producers. There were a few victualler brewers, publicans who brewed on their premises, who were not yet as significant as they became later in the seventeenth century. Then there were the home brewers.

In the first half of the seventeenth century there were no more than one or two victualler brewers at any one time.[205] William Baker was brewing at the Flying Horse, 24 West Street, for over 20 years and William Scott was brewing at what became the Castle, 76 West Street, in the 1640s. In 1649 Arthur Whitlocke was brewing at the Falcon, 1 West Street. One or two other brewers whose premises cannot be identified were probably also victualler brewers. Their presence was clearly not significant.

The incidence of home brewing, the third source of production of beer or ale, is more difficult to gauge.[206] Evidence of the importance of home brewing comes only from surviving household inventories. A random selection of 40 inventories (of 105 listed) for the ten years between 1639 and 1648 shows that 50% of those households had some sort of brewing equipment. 7 had brew houses, 2 had furnaces in the cellars and 11 had other implements, often in the kitchen. At the top of the scale Thomas Kennett, a gentleman and merchant of Faversham who died in 1639, had equipment valued at £4.3.0.[207] Lower down the scale John Savidge, a shipwright who died in 1639, had 9 beer vessels and 2 pails in his kitchen valued at 12/-.[208] John Berry, a collar maker who also died in 1639, had a furnace and a tub and earthenware beer pots valued at £1.19.0.[209] Ralph Payne a weaver, who also died in 1639 held 6 casks of beer in his buttery valued at 6/-.[210] Whilst it is a challenge to translate these figures into the absolute numbers of households who brewed at home, they do suggest that household brewing was widespread, in a way that the evidence does not suggest for the previous century.

These figures suggest a strong trend since the sixteenth century. Between 1565 and 1587 only 7% of inventories showed brewing equipment. 60 years later the households with brewing equipment had leap to 50%.[211] In other words for many households home brewing had became part of the home economy. This begs two questions. What were they brewing and why were they brewing at home? The answers to that may be no more than fashion, familiarity and cost. Once beer replaced ale as the normal drink, and not one inventory refers to ale, many understood that the process was simple and decided on grounds of cost, after start up, to produce a brew. The impact upon the common brewers would have been interesting. They were faced with competition, albeit from a very variable product.

The fourth source of beer in the previous century, imports, ceased by 1600. By then Faversham had become self sufficient in beer. Once the techniques of production had been mastered locally no more cargoes of beer came in to the port. Demand was satisfied by local producers.

In the sixteenth century demand for beer grew because of its increasing popularity, ie taste, allied to population growth. In the seventeenth century increasing demand depended upon population growth. Assuming that the population of Faversham and the immediately surrounding villages grew in proportion to that of the whole country,[212] [Table 9], in the first 50 years of the seventeenth century local population grew by 25%. In Faversham (Parish and Liberty), the population would have grown from about 1300 in 1550 to 1650 in 1600 and to 2050 in 1650. In the three immediately surrounding villages that Faversham would have supplied, of Ospringe, Preston and Davington, the population would have grown from about 325 in 1550, to 410 in 1600, and to 510 in 1650. To these numbers of daily drinkers has to be added a number for visitors, travellers and mariners in the town. That may have increased the town's population by 50 per day. In summary Faversham had to provide beer, or ale, each day for about 2100 people in 1600 and about 2610 people in 1650.

Using the same consumption figures as before, of an average of 8 pints per adult and 4 pints per child per day, the total production can then be estimated. That production was 16,000 barrels per annum in 1600 rising to 20,000 barrels in 1650.

To these figures has to be added the small quantities of beer that was exported. In 1600/1[213] Faversham sent beer to Calais, Flushing and Ostende in 14 cargoes, containing 7 pipes and 32 tuns of beer. That was a total of 284 barrels, less than 2% of the total home consumption. Of that total John Castlocke sent out 4 tuns and 2 pipes of beer, which totalled just 40 barrels. In 1611/12 the total amount of beer exported was only 16 barrels.[214] In 1621 about 130 barrels were sent abroad.[215] In 1625/6 only 2 tuns of beer were exported to Flushing.[216] No outwards coastal trade from Faversham in beer is recorded. Not only did the amounts exported fluctuate but over time they declined.

When the market shares are applied to the total production of beer, or ale, in Faversham the very modest outputs of each producer once again become obvious. If 50% of households brewed, either ale or beer and enough to satisfy their total requirements, that left 50% for the common brewers and the victualler brewers to share ie between 8,000 and 10,000 barrels of beer a year. From the evidence available in the Brewers Fines [Table 3] in 1625/6 there was only one victualler brewer, William Baker, with a share of 12 1/2%, or 1000 barrels output per year. By 1649 there were two known victualler brewers, John Clare and Arthur Whitlocke, and possibly two others, Richard Adrian and Francis Casse, with a combined share of 25% or 2500 barrels per year. The remainder was shared by the common brewers. Throughout the period the Castlockes, as common brewers, maintained their 25% share which grew from 2000 to 2500 barrels per year. The smallest brewers like the newcomer Thomas Baldock barely reached 400 barrels per year. The Castlocke market share of 25% sounds impressive, but translated into barrelage it is tiny by the standards of today.

Just as there were changes in production so there were changes in distribution. The common brewers continued to have a large private trade, which was direct to the customer, and which was still widespread well into the nineteenth century. What appears to have changed is the nascent 'tied trade' through public houses which were loosely connected to a brewer. In the early period the practice was growing but it had died out by the end of the century.

Of the 19 public houses licensed in 1601 there were 10 houses whose guarantors, or recognisances, were brewers (the Castlockes guaranteed 2) and 3 were maltsters (who traded with the Castlockes). 50% of the houses must have been supplied predominately by those brewers who were ready to guarantee, at their cost, the good behaviour of the licensees. In 1610, only 10 years later 18 licensees were issued and only 2 houses were guaranteed by a brewer and 2 by a maltster. This suggests that trade had become freer for whatever reason. [Table 6]. How this pattern changed by 1650 is unknown, as comparable records do not exist again until 1691. By then no brewers were guarantors. How this converts to barrelage is likewise impossible to say.

The numbers of inns, alehouses and tippling houses in Faversham grew during the period. In 1601 there were 19 and by 1662 there were 30, [Tables 6 & 7]. This 50% growth clearly outstripped the growth in local population. The quality of these houses was variable. Only 2 were called inns with inn keepers; the Ship and its neighbour in Market Place, the Fleur de Lys. None was held by a victualler. In 1601 the others were licensed to a variety of tradesmen ranging from a miller, a tailor, a butcher, a cooper, a barber and a minstrel, John Hutchens. By 1610 the profile of licensees had changed again. 5 were described as victuallers and 7 were described as widows. Thereafter comparable records have not survived until 1691, when all were described as victuallers. This suggests that more public houses were being run by dedicated licensees rather than a variety of people for whom victualling was not a full time occupation.

The location of only a half of the licensed houses can be identified precisely. These were the more important ones which had a name and survived for some time in one place. Smaller licensed houses came and went and these may never have had a name. The oldest houses were still in the commercial centre of Faversham, [Table 5], especially around the Market Place. Here were the Ship, the Fleur de Lys, the Horne, the Queens Arms and the Bear; all established before 1532.[217] Other long established houses were further out; the Anchor was at 25 Court Street, the Rose and

George was at 80 Preston Street, the Crowne was at 114 West Street and the Bell was at 37/38 Preston Street.

There was continuity of place but not of ownership of licensed houses. They were rarely tied to any interests or one family but were commercial assets that were bought and sold within each generation. Take as examples the three main central houses.[218] The Ship, 16 Market Place, in 1604 was owned by William Finch and lately by Hawkes. It was owned subsequently by Edward Hales and in 1653 was owned by William Dix, a successor to John Castlocke at the Brewery. The Fleur de Lys, next door at 15 Market Place, in 1604 was owned by Edward Murfield and lately by John Skyres. It was owned subsequently by John Greenstreet and Anne his wife, then John Crux and in 1653 by his heirs. The Horne, at 7 & 7A Market Place, was the exception. It was owned in 1604 by Margaret Owre widow and previously by her husband Alexander. It was owned subsequently by Boyce Owre and in 1653 by his heirs.

Continuity of tenancy was likewise short. As in previous years tenancies lasted longest for the best quality houses, which presumably produced the best returns. The Ship, at 16 Market Place, in the most central position with both rear access and a large yard for stabling is the best example. Thomas Saunders was tenant by 1590 and his widow replaced him in 1606. Gyles Ledgegood was tenant at the Queens Arms, a few houses east, by 1601 and he died there in 1611. None of the other tenants of houses in 1601 were still there ten years later.[219]

The sources of the ingredients of beer, malt and hops, varied as in the previous century. The supply of malt was entirely local and more even than that of hops. The production of barley, from which malt was made, was less susceptible to fluctuation than the production of hops. There were bad harvests but barley was sown each year, not so susceptible to bad weather and not susceptible to disease. Hop bines had to be nurtured over several years, they were susceptible to disease and to the weather.

As there was a strong trade from Faversham to London of malted barley and as no shipments inwards are recorded,[220] Faversham brewers must have been self sufficient in local malt. Hops were a different matter. Throughout the period there was a fluctuating inwards and outwards trade in hops. In 1601/2 John Castlocke sent out 2 bags of hops to Calais[221] and others sent out 4 pockets of hops to Calais and Flushing. Between February and July 1612[222] Faversham imported 19 bags of hops totalling 51 cwt.[223]

Using the multiples of 1830, (albeit much later but when statistics are available),[224] that would have produced 1250 barrels or 7% of local needs. In 1621 and 1627 small quantities of hops were imported from Wishing.[225] In 1628 8 bags of hops were sent out. In 1643/4 approximately 43 bags or 86 cwt. of hops were sent up to London[226] in Faversham boats by the Faversham merchants,

Thomas Knowler, John Jones, John Preston, John Fearne and William Dix. Of interest is the hop merchant William Dix. He was described as a merchant in malt, wheat and oats; he owned the Ship Inn; and was described as a servant of John Castlocke in his will and took over the running of the Castlocke Brewery in 1649. No better example of a small general merchant/entrepreneur dealing in interrelated activities in a prosperous port and market town could be found. In times of good harvests surpluses were sent out and after bad harvests hops were imported. Faversham's economy was part of a regional economy.

This evidence suggests that in or around Faversham, on that fine brick earth so suitable for hop growing, hop gardens had become established by the mid seventeenth century; but where were they, how large were they and who were the hop growers? Taking the first questions, the first reference to hop growing in Faversham is in 1590 at Homestall Farm.[227] The next, but oblique, reference to hop growing is in 1640. Francis Windsor, the brewer at the Standard, owned 'a load of hop poles' at his death.[228] These were valued at 10/-; which means about 125 poles for about 40 hills of hops, probably near his brewery.

An alternative answer to the question may be suggested by using 'back projection' from the presence of extensive hop gardens a century later, in 1750.[229] In the centre of Faversham, stretching south, west and east from the rear of Preston Street and West Street to London Road and Ospringe, in two large areas called Kingsfield and Cooksditch Farm were 40 acres of hop gardens. A century earlier, in 1653,[230] the owners of Kingsfield were Faversham's leading brewers; John Castlocke's heirs and William Tomlin, John Finch, whose family had brewing associations, and the victualler brewer John Greenstreete. In 1653 John Castlocke's heirs were by far the largest owners, followed by Finch, Greenstreet and Tomlin. In 1660 Maple Maplisden was the tenant but he was growing barley there. This suggests that not only were the Castlockes the leading brewers of Faversham but that they may have been local hop growers who invested in protecting their supply of that expensive and unreliable crop.

The product of beer continued to be classified as either strong or weak beer, but within these two categories the quality must have been far from consistent. Technology, of even the simple thermometer, was non-existent. Brews depended entirely upon the experience of the brewers concerned.

Price and quality continued to be controlled nominally nationally but in practice by the Faversham Corporation. Each year the Corporation nominated two ale conners to inspect each brew. Considering that rarely any of those nominated were brewers or victuallers, or remained in place for more than a year, the quality control must have been cursory. In 1625 and 1626/7,[231] Chatborne Arrow, a glover and victualler in 1610 and John Cruttall, a baker and a guarantor of

Mrs. Ledgegood at the Queens Arms in 1610,[232] were exceptions. Suspected infringements, of the Assize of Bread and Ale, were reported by the presenters appointed each year for each street by the Corporation.

These infringements were dealt with by the mayor sitting in a semi judicial capacity. Cases were common. In 1602 for example John Castlocke the common brewer was fined 12d and Edward Wilson the common brewer was fined 2d.[233] In the same year William Tomlin and Robert Hilton, also common brewers, were fined 12d each for 'breaking the assize against the form of the statute'. Victuallers and innkeepers were dealt with in the same way by the Corporation. In a small town where gossip and tittle-tattle were endemic reasonable quality must have been encouraged.

In 1606 the Faversham Market Court was held before the mayor and dealt with 39 cases.[234] The price of beer was set for the brewers at 8/- for a barrel of Best (or Strong) Beer and 4/8 for a barrel of Small Beer. The four brewers John Castlocke, William and Robert Hilton and William Tomlin were each presented for selling beer above 2d per gallon. The two innkeepers, Gyles Ledgegood and Widow Saunders were presented for miss selling oats. 33 victuallers were presented for selling with stone pots or kans unsealed.

In addition to beer, and ale, one other drink was beginning to appear in Faversham; that was wine. The Faversham Port Books show a number of small imports in the late sixteenth century. There were probably imports before this time as in 1567/8 wine shipments, originating from Rouen, Bordeaux and Calais, from the other Kent ports of Dover, Maidstone and Rochester, were arriving in London.[235] In the early seventeenth century imports of French and a little Spanish wine, usually from Flushing to Faversham, shot up.

In 1615/16[236] there were 26 inwards shipments to Faversham of 82 hogsheads, 4 butts and 20 tuns of wine, which totalled 412 barrels. Whilst this equalled 10,700 wine gallons or 85,000 pints or approximately 425,000 glasses of wine, a seemingly huge amount, it is not inconceivable this was consumed locally, but it is probably unlikely. An estimated adult population of 1000 could easily have drunk a glass and a quarter of wine a day, but the elite 10% of the population, who would have been the only ones able to afford wine, is unlikely to have drunk two bottles of wine a day, albeit a weak wine. Some of this wine must have been drunk locally; some probably came into Whitstable, the sub customs port of Faversham, for Canterbury; some may have been sent overland to Ashford for the Weald; and some must have been shipped on to London. Without that there would have been a substantial cultural shift from beer drinking that is not documented locally elsewhere.

In the following decades the imports of wine were much lower. In 1627/8[237] only 72 barrels (17000 pints) of wine came into Faversham from overseas. The same cargoes included 400 dozen earthen bottles covered in wicker. This suggests that wine was bottled locally for a retail trade. These 4800 bottles would have bottled a little under a half of the cargoes but if they were reused would have been sufficient to bottle the whole cargo. In 1634/5[238] only 87 barrels of wine came into Faversham from overseas. These figures seem to reflect more accurately the gradually developing drinking fashion of Faversham before the Civil War.

The commercial activities of some of the brewers extended beyond brewing but were related to it. John Castlocke III, before taking over the brewery of his father at 18 Court Street, had a number of interests that would have prepared him for the business. In 1596 he is described as a yeoman[239] which suggest he had some farming interests. In 1600 he is described as a maltster[240]. In 1602 he is described as an inn holder and later as a 'badger'[241]. A badger was licensed by two or more Justices of the Peace annually as a wholesaler who could buy corn or victuals in one place and carry them to sell in another. There is little record of him trading through the port which suggests his trade was by road. This in turn suggests that his activities were local.

The public lives of the brewers in the seventeenth century followed those of the previous century. According to their status in the commercial hierarchy they progressed, all things being equal, up the Corporation hierarchy. The stepping stones to the mayoralty were set. Starting with becoming a freeman, so that one could trade in the town and so become an elector of the Faversham Corporation, led to becoming a common councillor then for fewer men one of the limited number of jurats and then for a very few men a mayor.

The Hiltons for example, as lesser brewers, never became mayors but did fulfil lesser roles in public life. In 1617 John Hilton became a common councillor and in 1627 an auditor of the finances of the Corporation. By the time of his death in 1628 he was a jurat.[242] By 1632 Richard Hilton was a commoner and in 1638 a jurat. In 1640 he was Governor of the Grammar School and in 1643 Governor of the Almshouses.[243] Two other lesser brewers, John Scott and John Greenstreete, each became common councillors. Scott became the town auditor in 1628. Their remuneration was in kind, by access to the purchase of small numbers of leases of town property or rights, at beneficial rates. In the case of John Hilton remuneration was the 21 years lease of the Town Droits in 1626 and for John Greenstreete the lease of the same in 1645. At a date when the only paid borough officer was the town clerk, the only part paid officer was the mayor, and when there were no civil servants, the running of the town depended upon such annually elected unpaid townsmen.

John Castlocke III became the mayor of Faversham in 1628, as did the other substantial brewer William Tomlin in 1618. They too had a record of service. John III was an auditor in 1605, 1610, 1611; a chamberlain in 1606; and a receiver of Trowtes land in 1609. John Castlocke IV was the

Governor of the House of Correction in 1640 and the Governor of the Town Stock for the Poor in 1646. Their 'remuneration' was the lease of Brook Farm in Sussex for 21 years from 1609 at an annual rent of £100 plus an entry fine of £100. In 1623 £200 was lent to them and in 1632 a further £200 was lent them for one year for re lending to an unnamed Teynham brewer.[244] This appears to be an example of a commercial credit. These arrangements were much more substantial than those of Hilton and Greenstreet.

An example of the work John Castlocke III did for the commercial affairs of the town appears in 1616. The Corporation, on his initiative, drew up new Ordinances for the Regulation of Tradesmen. The Mercers Company was established, which was to include brewers, inn holders and vintners It cannot have been coincidence that John III was the first Master and Freeman. A new trade regulatory body was founded by the leading businessman of the town and survived into the nineteenth century.

The office of mayor in seventeenth century Faversham was not merely honorific. The mayor was chief magistrate but as such was less a criminal judge than an arbitrator over a wide range of petty local largely administrative disputes. He made the decisions on the implementation of the Borough bye laws. It was a demanding and time consuming position. 1602 provides a near complete example of the work involved.[245] Whilst this was not during the mayoralty of a Castlocke it illustrates what he would have done during his mayoralty.

He chaired the monthly meeting of the Council or Court of Wardmote, frequently charged with implementing government policy dictated by the Lord Warden of the Cinque Ports or the Lord Lieutenant of the County.

He chaired the Sessions of the Peace and Goal Delivery 'to hear and determine all felonies, trespasses, falsehoods, contempts and pleas of the Crown in the town as well as goal delivery of prisoners in the town'. In 1602 there were hundreds of petty presentments. Many concerned obstruction of roads, noisome gutters, providing artillery or committing an affray. Most concerned the breaking of the Assize of Bread or Beer or Ale. In Preston Street 8 victuallers were fined for breaking the Assize of Bread and fined between 4d and 12d each. In West Street 8 had broken the Assize of Beer, 3 the Assize of Ale, 1 the Assize of Beer and Ale, 3 the Assize of Bread and 2 the Assize of Beer and Bread; and were fined likewise. In Court and Abbey Street the common brewers John Castlocke and Edward Wilson, and 10 common victuallers were fined between 2d and 5d for breaking the Assize.

The Mayor chaired the Court of Portmote, for 43 sessions, for which there are 185 files, between April 1601 and December 1602. These cases concerned debt, trespass, gavelkind, property and rent. He chaired the monthly Court for Withernams for which there are 120 files for the same period. He presided over 3 sittings in July and October to agree property transfers by Feet of Fine. The Mayor granted the Recognisances to the inn keepers, tipplers and victuallers and he took dozens of Views of Frankpledge. All these functions gave the Mayor considerable opportunity to influence the affairs of the town.

The private lives of the brewers are difficult to follow as not one personal paper of any of them has survived. The only insight into family lives is through marriages and children. [Castlocke Pedigree]. They all married locally and often several times. John Castlocke II married the daughter of a leading townsman. John Castlocke III married firstly the daughter of another Faversham brewer, Thomas Cole, and secondly the daughter of an Isle of Harty yeoman, and subsequent Faversham townsman and mayor, Samuel Hayward. John Castlocke IV married also the daughter of a Harty yeoman. Surviving children remained local, with the exception of Daniel Castlocke who moved to the City of London to become a Citizen and Grocer by 1612.

The Castlocke/Hayward marriages must have caused especial interest in the 1620s and were lampooned in the eighteenth century press.[246] The verse ran:

My father is my son
And I am my mother's mother
My sister is my daughter
I'm grandmother to my brother.

John III remarried the step daughter of his own daughter, (his step grand-daughter) who was 30 years his junior. When widowed she in turn re-married, a relation of the old Stransham brewing family, Richard Masters. John was clearly a remarkable man, not least because he lived to be 76. John IV married his sisters step daughter, a sister of his father's second wife.

There was no better sign of the social, commercial and municipal successes of the Castlockes than the grant of arms to John Castlocke III on 10th August 1614. He was described as 'gentleman whose ancestor inhabited Faversham by reason of John their uncle who was Lord Abbot of the Monastery there'.[247] He joined the armigerous families of his kinsmen and fellow townsmen, Hayward and Stransham. Consolidation of the family position was recognised and seemed assured. Within a generation it had all gone.

The early seventeenth century brewers of Faversham were relatively men of substance but their individual life time achievements were varied. There was a hierarchy of achievement at death, as shown in their wills and probate inventories, as there was in life.

At the lower end of the scale Robert Hilton and John Hilton, who died in 1628, left modest amounts.[248] They were second generation brewers. William Tomlin, a mayor of Faversham who died in 1619 left nearly £400 in cash plus a brewery and a house in Preston Street.[249] He was a quasi second generation brewer through his father in law. At the top of the scale were the Castlockes. Not only did their wills show them as more successful brewers than the others, but by comparison of three generations we can determine if they merely maintained their wealth or improved on their patrimony. Here was a commercial family of third, fourth and fifth generation common brewers.

John Castlocke II died in 1613. In his will, which was proved in the Archdeacons Court of Canterbury, he bequeathed a large estate. In cash he left £450, an unspecified residue and an annuity of £47.6.8 per annum, which equated to a capital value of about £1000. In real estate he left his brewery and house at 18 Court Street; a house in Market Place; 4 houses in Church Lane; 3 houses, garden and a malt house in Middle Row; and a house with barn, orchard and 3 acres in Preston Street west.[250]

His son, John Castlocke III, died in 1651. In his will, which was proved in the superior Prerogative Court of Canterbury. In cash he left £110, an undisclosed residue and money for apprenticeships for the poor in Faversham. In household goods he left both silver and pictures. In real estate he left Morrisse Court and farm in Bapchild, Rodmersham and Tong; lands called Finners, Chilson Marsh and a house and 10 acres in the Isle of Harty; and in Faversham the brewery, and taken from other sources 3 houses in Court Street East or Middle Row, a barn and lands in Preston Street West and 3 houses plus gardens and land in West Street.[251] This was an estate which was probably comparable to his father's but not one which suggests a significant increase in wealth.

One year later in 1652 his son, John Castlocke IV, died. His will was also proved in the superior court; a subtle commentary upon the social progress of the family, but not necessarily the 'wealth progress' of the family, since 1613. He left only £57 in cash plus an undisclosed residue. In real estate he left The Brewery, a property called the Ship on the Keys and about 50 acres of land at Kingsfield in Faversham. The property in Middle Row and Court Street East had been sold by 1653.The balance of the property left by his father was probably still in the lifetime interest of his mother.[252] Brewing even at the top end in a small town like Faversham was hardly the route to ever increasing wealth. As his only child, John Castlocke V, had died in infancy in 1632, the death of John Castlocke IV brought the family in the male line to an abrupt end.

Four years earlier, in 1648, brewing by John Castlocke had been brought to an equally dramatic end, by politics. The confrontation of the King and Parliament and the ensuing Civil War had directly affected Kent and Faversham.[253] Fines and imprisonments followed the failure of the rising in 1643, when a rendezvous of the moderates and Royalists was planned for Faversham, and the Vicar of Faversham was ejected and replaced by a Puritan. In 1648 The Kent County Petition, signed or supported by thousands, reopened festering divisions and led to the Kent

Revolt in 1648. One of the county magazines was captured in Faversham and Fairfax's Army poured down the London road to re take Canterbury. National events impinged directly upon the lives of the people of Faversham.

Political purges of municipal elites followed. In November 1648 the Faversham Corporation removed 7 Jurats; that was half of the most senior members of the Corporation. John Castlocke, Boys Owre, Thomas Napleton, Nathaniel Besbeech, John Knowler, John Preston and Nicholas Wade, 'late Jurats of the Town for being in commission against the new parliament in this late insurrection and for other means against the peace of this Town shall be displaced and disfranchised of every office and no longer to sit on the Bench as Jurats nor to be any longer free in the said Town.' John Castlocke was doubly tainted by his cousins the Pordages of Ospringe and Rodmersham who were Roman Catholic.[254] To be removed from the bench was sustainable but to lose the freedom of the town was not. His commercial rights were removed. He was barred from brewing and trading.

After 150 years of being at the centre of the life of Faversham the Castlocke family simply disappeared; much as the Shepherd family did in 1876. Today they are remembered only by the fine monument to John III in the north transept of the Faversham Parish Church and by Castlocke Street, built on ground they once owned. What did survive was their brewery.

## CHAPTER FIVE

# Survival and Recovery under the Baldocks and the Marshes: 1650-1732

After the uncertainty of the Civil War and the Commonwealth, brewing in Faversham over the next 80 years was characterised by periodic uncertainty, polarisation and then consolidation. Until 1685 the industry comprised one large common brewer and an ever increasing number of very small brewers and victualler brewers. Thereafter the industry saw the near disappearance of the victualler brewer and the emergence of two substantial common brewers, Richard Marsh and Alexander Bax. From these descended directly the two Faversham breweries which faced each another across Court Street until 1990: Shepherd Neame and Rigden/Fremlin/Whitbread. Home brewing followed a similar pattern of decline. Distribution continued to be through private trade and an ever increasing number of public houses, whose numbers shot up out of proportion to the modest rise in population, and then in turn declined. From 1700 the practice of brewers buying tied houses to protect their sales outlets became permanently established. Consolidation of the sector was producing an industry recognisable today.

At the most substantial brewery the pressing problem for the Castlocke family was to keep it going in changed circumstances. As a temporary measure the running of the business was entrusted to the 'old servant' William Dix. With the death of John Castlocke III in 1651, followed one year later in 1652 by that of his son and then the death of Dix in 1653 the future became more uncertain. The situation was exacerbated by family dispute. In his will John Castlocke IV left The Brewery to his distant kinsman by marriage Thomas Hilton of Sittingbourne, possibly because he had some brewing knowledge as the son of a previous Faversham brewer, John Hilton. John's widow Abigail contested her husband's will and joined with his sister Barbara Bourne and his cousin Mary Knowler to bring a suit. Chancery issued a writ for the production of deeds and the will but the case never came to trial.[255]

Thomas gained possession of The Brewery in 1654 but the uncertainty continued. He ran the business for five years and then he died. His widow carried on for a year [Table 3] but neither of his sons, another Thomas[256] and his brother Castlocke Hilton, who were young children in 1659, became brewers. They retained the ownership of the property but leased it. Yet again premature death intervened. The new tenant brewer in 1660, Mildmay Maplisden, who came from Charing and Maidstone, died within a year.[257] [258] Fortune then turned, with irony, in the form of Thomas Baldock.

Thomas Baldock was not a native of Faversham but appeared here by 1644. From a small start he built up his knowledge of brewing and the trade. By 1660 he was the most experienced brewer, and had been in business longer than any other brewer in Faversham. Unexpectedly his competition had disappeared. A big gap had opened up in the market place. Whether he seized the opportunity or widow Hilton came to him to run her family major asset is debatable. It was however ironic that he should have saved the old Brewery. Just as the Royalist, Castlocke, had been stripped of his civic rights in 1648, so Baldock, a Commonwealth man, was stripped of his right to vote as a Faversham Commoner in 1660.[259] Despite that disability, he and his family carried on the business successfully for 18 years as the major common brewers in Faversham.

Thomas Baldock died in 1667,[260] after nearly 25 years of brewing in Faversham. His widow carried on for a year and then their younger son, James Baldock, took over.[261] He died 7 years later and was commemorated in the Faversham Parish Church by an ironical inscription on his grave stone.[262] It read:

Here lyth the bodie of James
Baldock Brewer of this Towne
who died 8 February 1673
aged 33 years

A man once flourishing
like the laurel tree,
but soon cut downe
by death in his prosperity.

For 3 years brewing passed again to a widow, Amy Baldock, and then for 1 year to her second husband, Edward Chapman. In 1678 that came to an end. Once again mortality forced a change in occupancy. James Baldock left two infant daughters when he died, who could take no part in running a brewery for at least 15 years,[263] and his widow's second husband probably followed him soon after. Yet another new man arrived to brew. With the coming of Richard Marsh stability returned to the Brewery for the next 50 years.

Whilst the family background of Richard Marsh is known, his reason for coming to Faversham is unclear. [Marsh Pedigree].[264] The Marsh family was an old Kent gentry family which had been settled at East Langdon near Deal from the Middle Ages and later at Brandred, Acrise. The family then moved to the Old Court, Nonnington and finally to Nethersole House, Womenswold, also near Deal, after Richard's father, John Marsh, became the sole heir to his maternal uncle, Sir Francis Nethersole (1587-1659).[265] Here was the source of some wealth, but Richard was the fourth of five sons so unlikely to have inherited any major family property.

Clearly Richard had to find a career. Through the intimate world of East Kent and farming and malting near Sandwich, which had close trading links with Faversham, he must have heard of the unexpected opportunities at the town's leading brewery. It is possible the introduction was direct through his relation Thomas Marsh of Langdon and the Master family also of Langdon.[266] Whether he had any brewing training is unknown. He probably had to rely upon a few brewery servants and the monopoly position in the short term. The future of the brewery was far from stable in 1678 for here was an owner and then his heirs, his mortgagees and his tenant. By 1672 Thomas Hilton junior had mortgaged the brewery at 18 Court Street to John Castlocke's relations by marriage, Robert Master Esq. and John Knowler.[267] By 1680 Hilton was dead and the mortgage had been taken over by William Dix junior.[268] Richard's entry into The Brewery was gradual. In 1678 he was the tenant brewer of Thomas Hilton or his heir.[269] By 1689 he was the tenant brewer and mortgagee of the Hilton heir.[270] By 1711 he was owner, occupier and brewer.[271] These were the classic steps of buying gradually into a business.

Starting at the age of 28, Richard Marsh senior was brewing in Faversham for nearly 50 years. By 1705[272] his youngest son, another Richard by then only 18, was at The Brewery. Richard senior died in 1726 aged 76. He was succeeded by Richard junior but within a year he too was dead aged 40. leaving an infant daughter, Silvester, and a widow, Mary. Once again the business was left to a young widow and an infant child. Uncertainty returned.

At the same time that Richard Marsh was consolidating his brewery another new brewer arrived in Faversham: Alexander Bax. He was of the same generation as Richard Marsh and like him he came from a village behind Deal, Ash, but he came from a different background. His father was a modest tenant farmer and his family were village blacksmiths.[273] He was born in 1654 and first appears as a brewer in Faversham in 1685.[274] [Table 3]. He too was the youngest son aged 29 when he established himself here. He was left a modest patrimony in his father's will of only £70 and the year before he arrived in Faversham he had married Susan Smith, the daughter of a Sandwich farmer. His inheritance and a marriage settlement probably provided just enough capital to set up a new plant. The farming, malting and coastal trade networks of Sandwich, Faversham and East Kent provided the route. Nothing is known of his brewing training but his enterprizing personality provided the drive to break into a long established sector in Faversham. What is interesting in his case is that he set up a new brewery on a new site and did not take over an existing business.

Continuation of the Bax brewery was threatened by the early death of Alexander in 1702, aged 48, and the death of his wife in the following year. His two sons, Stephen and Alexander, aged 9 and 13 were not at an age to take over the business and no brewing trustees were appointed to run it until they were.[275] The brewery did survive, for it was either leased to or run by Edward Weller.[276] Alexander junior died unmarried in 1710 and Stephen who inherited the brewery premises was described in his 1712 Marriage Licence as a beer brewer.[277] He never carried on the business, withdrew from Faversham for some years and followed the life of a gentleman, with income generated by his father's properties.

Edward Weller carried on the Bax brewery and was described as a brewer until at least 1749.[278] He was yet another new comer to Faversham, whose introduction to the town can only be conjectured. He was born about 1678 into an old Rolvenden family,[279] and was under 30 when he arrived in Faversham. He brewed here for at least 40 years and was buried in the Faversham Parish Church aged 84 in 1762.[280] Through him Faversham's other long lasting brewery, the Rigden Brewery, emerged. William Rigden, from Canterbury, was listed as his 'servant' in 1739.[281] Edward Rigden, also from Canterbury, was listed as a Faversham brewer in 1749[282] and as the occupier of the Bax brewery in 1769.[283] Ambitious young men from outside Faversham were continually drawn to profitable opportunities offered by the town.

The brewing premises from which these men operated were spread through the town and some changed during the period. Thomas Baldock started modestly in the old premises of Robert Hilton at 88/90 West Street and from 1660 may have brewed at 15/17 Preston Street, the old Tomlin site, at the same time as brewing at 18 Court Street.[284] His son James and his widow Amy Baldock brewed at 18 Court Street, as did his successors the Marshes, and Shepherd Neame Ltd continue to do today. Technologies were transferred through the transfer of old sites. For Bax it was different. He set up a new brewery on a new site at 67/68 Preston Street. There is no clue to why he chose this site as it had no previous connection with brewing.[285] Possibly the water table, as in other parts of Preston Street, was near the surface. Edward Weller occupied the site as the tenant of Stephen Bax and it continued to be described as having a' brew house, malt house, mill house and buildings' in the occupation of Edward Rigden as late as 1769.[286]

These were the major common brewers during the period, but what were their market shares? Whilst no business records survive, their relative output can be deduced from the Brewers Fines, listed annually in the Faversham Wardmote Books until 1699. The Baldocks and the Marshes dominated production. In 1660 Thomas Baldock paid 37% of the total Fine collected by the town. By 1666 this share had risen to 57% of the total and then fell back to 40%. Richard Marsh continued the predominance of a single brewer. In 1678 his share was 42% and peaked in 1693/4 at 62%, the highest ever market share of one brewer in Faversham. It is also interesting that within a year of arrival Alexander Bax was paying 25% of the total Fine and by 1698 he was paying 30% of the total Fine collected by the town. After the arrival of Bax the two largest Faversham brewers probably produced 80% of the brewers capacity of Faversham. The remaining 20% was spread amongst a number of small producers.

After 1660 the brewing sector in Faversham polarised at the top end and fragmented below, before contracting sharply. [Table 3]. In the 1660s the numbers of brewers fluctuated around 12; in the 1670s the numbers fluctuated around 19; in 1678 they peaked at 24; by 1686 they fell to 9; and in 1699 stood at 6. By the 1730s they had dropped further. At the peak the 10 smallest brewers were paying less than 1 1/2% of the total Fine. Their production was marginal.

This secondary and fragmenting source of production was composed of victualler brewers, or publicans who brewed on their premises. In 1649 there were 4 known victualler brewers who accounted for 40% of the total numbers of brewers but 18% of total output. In 1663 there were 10 victualler brewers who accounted for 80% of the numbers of brewers but for 55% of total brewing output. In 1691 there were 6 victualler brewers who accounted for 66% of numbers but only 17% of total brewing output. [Tables 3 & 5].[287] Until 1707, when he died, one significant victualler brewer did survive. Thomas Higgs was the last of a type. Surprisingly, the average numbers of years these small brewers survived remained static at around 8 years throughout the period.

The premises of the victualler brewers were also spread through the town. In 1663 Henry Leese was brewing at the Dolphin in Preston Street; Rebecca Bentson was brewing at the Keys; John Clare was brewing at the Crowne at 116/118 West Street; Robert Hogben was brewing on the west side of Preston Street; and Frances Whitlocke was brewing at the Falcon, 1 West Street.[288] By 1691, when the numbers of victualler brewers had dropped, John Major was brewing at the Anchor in Abbey Street; John Thomas at the Bull in Tanners Street; Thomas Varham at the Sun in West Street; Nicholas Mockett at the Tun in West Street; Joanna Tanner at the Crowne in Abbey Street; and John Philpott at the unidentified Turks Head. Between 1700 and 1707 Thomas Higgs was brewing at both the Ship, in Market Place, and at the brew house attached to the Blue Anchor at The Standard Quay.[289]

The rise and fall of the victualler brewer was not unique to Faversham. Nationally, it has been calculated that in 1700 50% of beer for sale was produced by common brewers and 50% by victualler brewers.[290] The evidence for Faversham suggests that the trend here began and ended earlier. The local evidence also suggests that the timing of the arrival and continuation of two substantial brewers in a small town displaced the small independent producers earlier than elsewhere. The one exception was Thomas Higgs, who arrived and died after 7 years, at the very end of the period of victualler brewers. Statistically he was a 'flash in the pan'. Economies of scale and the superior quality of the product of big brewers would provide the reason for the decline. The reason for their rise in the first place is more difficult to explain. Clearly enough small producers thought it was sufficiently profitable to brew and that there was a gap in the market place that they could fill. Possibly rising demand induced them or an expansion of the numbers of public houses induced experimentation. Whatever the reason the phenomenon was short lived.

The third source of production was domestic brewing at home. This traditional source continued in the seventeenth century but declined sharply in the early eighteenth century in the town. In the villages, in country houses and farmhouses, it survived into the nineteenth century. Whilst the incidence and scale of home brewing in Faversham is based upon sampling of the inherently selective evidence of probate inventories that have survived, a trend does emerge.[291]

Home brewing was carried on in both domestic brew houses and within the house. Of the 36 inventories reviewed between 1660 and 1670, there are 12 references to a brew house and 11 to brewing equipment elsewhere. Of the 21 inventories reviewed between 1670 and 1680, there are 8 references to a brew house and 2 to brewing equipment elsewhere. Of the 13 inventories reviewed between 1690 and 1700, there are 2 references to a brew house and only 1 to brewing equipment elsewhere. This quantifies two trends; the falling incidence of home brewing over 40 years from 64% of inventory households to 23% of inventory households; and the even sharper fall in home brewing inside the house.

The domestic brew houses recorded were owned by the elite of the town. Most owners were described as gentlemen, or successful merchants, and the remainder were a maltster, a grocer , a shipwright and a seaman. John Trowtes, a leading agricultural merchant was described as an Esquire. Those who brewed within their homes tended to be men of lesser worth. Their brewing equipment was recorded in cellars, butteries and kitchens.

By the 1730s home brewing declined further. The evidence, which comes from insurance policies, which were increasingly purchased by property owners, show that between 1720 and 1740 only two brew houses, attached to private houses in Faversham, were insured by the Sun

Fire Insurance Office. In 1731 Robert Day insured his brew house, at 27 Court Street, and in 1732 Robert Lukyn insured his brew house.[292] As they were both surgeons this equipment may have been for their professional use. That is not to say that small scale home brewing did not continue in some domestic kitchens in a pot over the fire, but for that there is no data. Home brewing in the town, where it can be shown to have survived, had become a marginal part of the domestic economy by 1730.

In the countryside the larger houses had brew houses and the tradition of home brewing survived here longer than elsewhere. For example, at Lees Court, south of Faversham, the leading landowning family of George Sondes, Earl of Faversham, maintained a substantial brew house. They maintained smaller ones at their town farm, Abbey Farm,[293] and at their country farm at Eastry Parsonage.

The fourth, but potential only, source of the supply of beer, or ale, was by import, either by road or by sea. Given that brewing was highly localised until the railway age, as the products did not travel, it is unlikely that much came into the town by road. The same was true of imports by sea. From sample reviews of the inwards trade Port Books of Faversham between 1660 and 1694, no beer, or ale, was recorded as coming into the port.[294] Faversham was self sufficient in the production.

What was being imported to Faversham in increasing quantities was wine. 1663 is a good example.[295] Of the 162 inwards voyages to Faversham, from London, 19 contained cargoes of wine; Spanish, French, Canary and Rhenish wine with one consignment of 'Aquabite, strong waters' and one of brandy. These cargoes were all in Faversham registered vessels so were probably destined for Faversham only. Spanish Wine was the most popular, possibly because of the European political situation; 3 butts, 36 pipes, 8 hogsheads and 10 cases are listed. French wine came next with 3 pipes and 14 hogsheads. Canary wine came in 1 1/2 hogsheads. Rhenish wine came in 1 butt. There were 2 pipes, 3 hogsheads and 2 rundlets of unnamed wines. That totalled 230 barrels or nearly 6000 gallons of wine imported into Faversham in one year.

Port and Malaga wines were imported directly to Faversham from overseas. For example, in 1681 there were 5 inwards cargoes of port in Faversham vessels.[296] On 24 April 1682 is recorded 'In the Kings Warehouse, Faversham. Taken out of the John of Faversham. Master William Amys. Merchant, Joseph Edwards. 2 tuns and 2 hogs heads of port. 102 gallons of brandy.' Here was the trade in alcohol, that was competing with beer, described in operation.

To return to the brewers; just as there was a range of producers so there was a range of premises, brewing equipment and stock.[297] There was a hierarchy here but with polarisation from the major common brewers to the victualler brewers. There was little in between.

The top end of the industry was represented by The Brewery at 18 Court Street. The site was, and is still, a typical town mediaeval 'messuage or burgage plot'. It is about 50 feet wide and runs 200 feet back downhill from the street to what was the mud bank of the Creek, and is now North Lane. The plot is long and narrow.

The earliest description of the layout of this plot is in 1731, for Hilles Hobday, brewer and second husband of Mary Marsh, nee Bax.[298] On the street was the house; behind and at the end of that, on the left or south side of the plot, was the brew house and the mill house with stock and utensils. On the right or north side of and behind the house were the storehouses, malt house, kiln house, granaries and stable with stock and utensils. The yard was beyond that. All the buildings were constructed of timber and tile. This footprint of the past survives substantially unaltered today.

The earliest description of the house and contents of The Brewery is in 1673, for James Baldock.[299] The house was still a substantially mediaeval house which had been modernised, especially with fireplaces in most rooms, in the seventeenth century. There was a hall, parlour, parlour buttery and stairs, where the entrance hall, reception corridor and meeting room are today; and a kitchen and buttery, where the board room is today. Upstairs, on the first floor, were the best chamber, the red chamber, the parlour chamber and the green chamber. The men's servants chamber and the maids chamber were probably in the attics above that.

The outbuildings are listed but because the premises were leased from Thomas Hilton the fixtures, especially of the brew house, with the exception of a copper pump valued at £4.0.0, were not. The stock of James Baldock is listed in detail, which suggests that he died unexpectedly whilst brewing.

In the Yard
1 waggon and 1 beercart valued at £4
2 Horses valued at £8

In the Brewhouse
8 chalder of coal valued at £14

In the Outhouses
1 1/2 bags of hops valued at £10
150 quarters of malt valued at £150
60 quarters of barley valued at £60

500 barrels of strong beer upon tally valued at £250
40 barrels of small beer upon tally valued at £15

18 Tuns 1/2 of hogheads, pipes and butts valued at £7.4.0
10 lasts of barrels valued at £15
2 lasts of kilderkins and firkins valued at £1.16.0

Lower down the scale were the premises, brewery and brewing equipment of Alexander Bax at 67-68 Preston Street, which are described in his Probate Inventory[300] of January 1702. The brewing equipment is described in detail as he was the owner and occupier of his premises but no barrels of beer are listed, possibly because he had stopped brewing temporarily due to illness.

In and about The Brewhouse and Washhouse
1 Copper valued at £2.5.0
2 Tunns, 1 Under Back, 1 Float and 1 Tub valued at £9.10.0
8 Cool Backs, 1 Copper, 4 Shootes and 1 Pump valued at £23.4.0

31 Barrels, 12 Kilderkins and 8 Firkins valued at £3.7.0
4 Hogsheads, 28 Butts, 4 Stocks and Stillings valued at £5.13.6
25 Butts, 23 Barrels, 6 Kilderkins and 5 Firkins abroad valued at £6.2.4

In the Yard and Malthouse
127 Quarters of Malt valued at £104.2.0
Hops valued at £1.0.0

1 Bushel, 1 Scry and Malt Mill valued at £3.8.0
1 Dray valued at 10/-

One other detailed description of substantial brewing premises has survived for the period; that of Thomas Higgs, the short lived brewer and innkeeper at the Ship Inn, Market Place, and the Blue Anchor, Standard Quay, who died in 1707.[301] He was the only large victualler brewer. The inventory for the Ship describes his buildings, brewing equipment, and wine cellar stock. The inventory of the Anchor lists only moveable equipment, because he was a tenant. Neither lists a stock of beer, which suggests he too was unable to brew before he died due to illness.

At The Ship
In the Brewhouse
1 Large Copper and Bed of Irons, 2 Pumps, 3 Shoots, 3 Moake Skivers, 1 Iron Rack and 1 Iron Poker valued at £30.3.6
1 Mash Tun, 1 Liquor Back, 2 Wort Backs, 1 Float valued at £20.10.0
5 Liquor Shoots as they all stand, 2 Malt Baskets, 36 Birch Brooms, 1 Net, 1 Draining Tub and Keeler valued at £3.1.8
1 Guile Tun, 1 Pump, 1 Mill, 3 Old Backs, 1 Loading Plank valued at £18.12.6
4 Starting Tubs valued at £1.0.0
1 Leather Pipe valued at £1.5.0
3 Pair of Barrel Slings and 1 Pair of Hogshead Slings valued at 11/6

1 Bag of Hops of 200lbs. valued at £7.10.0
190 Seams of Malt and 10 Seams of Wheaten Malt valued at £240.0.0

195 Butts valued at £97.10.0
23 Hogsheads valued at £4.12.0

107 Barrels valued at £24.1.6
44 Half Barrels valued at £4.8.0
105 Firkins valued at £7.17.6
5 Pins valued at 5/-
5 Other Barrels valued at £1.2.6

1 Feather Bed and Blankets, 1 Wheel Barrow, 1 Bushel, 1 Fan, 1 Scry, 2 Scopes, 1 Old Oast Hair and 3 Locks valued at £2.3.0
12 Sacks valued at £1.0.0

In the Beer Cellar
1/2 Barrel of Beer in a Butt valued at 10/-

In the Wine Cellar
15 Gallons of Brandy valued at £6.15.0
28 Gallons of Canary Wine valued at £8.6.8
4 Gallons of Claret valued at £1.0.0
5 Gallons of Cherry Brandy valued at £2.0.0
4 Gallons of Cherry Brandy and Plaine in Bottles valued at £2.2.0

At The Blue Anchor at The Standard
1 Tun Tub, 1 Large Keeler, 1 Skiver, 1 Shoot, 1 Stalder and 1 Broad Ladder for the Quays valued at £1.1.6

A summary of these figures gives an indication of the relative sizes of the three large breweries in Faversham. By numbers of barrels (in use and empty combined); Baldock had 684, Bax had 310 and Higgs had 910. In malt values; Baldock had £150, Bax had £104 and Higgs had £240. By value of hops; Baldock had £10, Bax had £1 and Higgs had £7.10.0. By values of brewing equipment; Baldock had no figure, Bax had £34.19.0 and Higgs had £75.4.2. In beer stock value; Baldock had £290 and no figure is given for the others. For the first seven years of the eighteenth century Thomas Higgs appears to have been the biggest Faversham brewer, from the constricted site at the rear of a busy central inn and at a site near the Creek.

At the lowest level of the brewing industry were the victualler brewers. The descriptions and values of the brewing equipment and stock of these small operations show that there was a big gap between them and the three big common brewers.

Arthur Whitlocke,[302] of the Falcon, 1 West Street, in 1660, left a copper, backs and equipment valued at £13 and 12 barrels of beer and Canary wine valued at £10. Robert Davison of Preston Street West, in 1664, left brewing equipment valued at £12.10 0 plus 10 barrels of strong beer, a copper and 4 stalders valued at £6.10.0. John Clare of the Crowne, 116/118 West Street, in 1668 left brewing equipment valued at £16.14.6 plus 10 tuns and 29 barrels of beer valued at £18.17.0.

Thomas Borsley, of 8 or 10 Preston Street, in 1671, left brewing coppers and vessels valued at £15 and 12 barrels of strong beer valued at £7.14.0 plus other barrels valued at £2.8.6. Richard Foster of the Ship, in 1673, left brewing equipment valued at £11.0.0 plus casks and hogsheads valued at £5.0.0, 68 barrels of strong beer valued at £44 and wine valued at £152. John Fryer, of West Street south, left brewing equipment valued at £13 and barrels and casks valued at £16. Vincent Hills, possibly of the Dolphin, Preston Street, in 1673, left a copper, mash tun, guile tun, 4 water tubs, a jet, 2 cool backs, barrels and bottles valued at £6.15.0 plus beer in his cellar valued at £3.5.0. Andrew Bell, in 1677, left in the brew house, a copper, mash tun, brewing tun, 2 backs, wort pump, 2 shoots, 2 rangs, 2 hinges, 1 bucking tub, 1 bar tub, 1 coop, 1 jet, 3 wort keelers , 1 little copper and 2 pails valued at £11 plus, in the cellar, 39 barrels of strong beer, hogsheads, pipes, barrels valued at £34.9.0.

Edward Tanner, in 1687, left a brewing tun, backs and equipment valued at £8 plus 9 barrels of strong beer valued at £5.8.0 and casks valued at £1.6.0. William Varham and his wife, of the Bear in Market Place, in 1689 and 1690 left a copper, tuns and backs valued at £5.2.7 plus 17 barrels of beer in the cellar valued at £13.6.4.

The average values of the brewing equipment of these victualler brewers is £11, with a maximum value of £16 and minimum of £5. The average value of stock listed is £10, leaving aside the special stocks of Richard Foster at the Ship.

These figures help to confirm the range of market shares of the common brewers and the victualler brewers suggested by the Brewers Fines.[303] They are especially helpful because they are drawn from an independent source. £10 worth of stock is far below the £290 of stock of James Baldock; it is barely 3%.

Further still down the scale of brewing in Faversham are those brewing at home for domestic consumption. Only one was of size; John Trowtes, Esquire, at 23 Court Street. In 1675 his brew house contained 2 coppers, 3 tuns, 1 cool back, 2 bucking tubs, 1 wash bowl, 11 small tubs, 1 ring, 2 stalders and 1 pair of weights.[304] At a valuation of £15 this equipment compared to that of the victualler brewers. Between 1660-1680 the average value of equipment in domestic brew houses was £3.15.0 and less elsewhere.[305]

In the countryside the tradition of home brewing continued, and in the case of the Sondes family on a substantial scale. In 1677 the brew house at their main house, Lees Court, Sheldwich, contained 'two coppers, brewing vessels and materials belonging to them' which were valued at £35.[306] In the Cellar were 'hogheads and barrels, a cider press, the stillings and 20 dozen glass bottles' valued at £10. At their Abbey Farm in Faversham in the brew house were '1 great furnace, 1 little furnace, 1 tun, 1 tub, 2 keelers, 4 hogsheads, 4 barrels, 1 kilderkin, 1 firkin, 1 half firkin and a cheese press' valued at £10. At their Parsonage Farm at Eastry their brew house contained '1 copper, tubs and keelers, 1 tun, bucking tubs and other vessels for brewing' valued at £5.12.0. The value of some of this equipment made the potential brewing operations of Sondes comparable to that of one of the leading Faversham common brewers, Alexander Bax.

The range of products that all these brewers produced changed little from previous periods. There was strong beer, small beer, ale and whatever domestic concoction home brewers contrived. Common and victualler brewers production was still regulated by the Faversham Corporation's Assize of Bread Beer and Ale, and still exercised by the ale conners. They controlled quality and price and there was no incentive to or possibility of introducing new product ranges. With the variety of water sources the taste of the beer of each brewer must have varied. Perhaps this differentiated the beer of each brewer so much that there was no need to experiment with new product ranges.

The question of how far hopped beer had replaced un-hopped ale is still difficult to answer. From the evidence of the probate inventories the impression is that the production of ale had disappeared entirely. Ale is not listed once in the hundreds of documents reviewed, but barrels of both strong and small beer frequently are. This impression is enforced by the description of the brewing equipment listed; it is more sophisticated than would be needed for ale. On the other hand hops are never listed, perhaps because they were deemed a grocery. For lack of quantifiable data one is left with the impression that ale or a non-hopped malt drink was produced, if at all, in a pot over the kitchen fire only in the poorer houses, at least in Faversham.

Such was the structure of the Faversham brewing industry but what was the demand for beer during this period and what was influencing that demand? Transport of beer over dreadful roads was still an obstacle to the delivery of a stable product beyond the three immediate villages. Shipping beer to London or around the coast never developed, for there is no evidence in the Port Books to show more than a very occasional shipment of a few barrels. Demand continued to depend on local population and visitors to Faversham

Between 1650 and 1700 national population fell by 5%, then recovered and then increased by about 10% by 1725.[307] Assuming the population of Faversham and the three surrounding villages of Ospringe, Preston and Davington, followed that pattern, and was spread as in 1801,[308] that gives the Faversham population of 2050 and the villages population of 510, or 2560 in total, in 1650; 2430 in 1675; 2560 in 1700; and 2820 in 1725. To these have to be added visitors and mariners, possibly an average net inflow of 50 per day to a port and market town.

Assuming that the entire population continued to drink an average of 6 pints of beer or ale per day, Faversham had to brew 20,000 barrels in 1650, falling to 19,000 in 1675, rising to 20,000 barrels in 1700 and to 22,000 barrels in 1725. Substitution of other drinks had barely begun. Wines were still too expensive for most people; gin drinking did not develop until the 1730s; and tea and coffee was still unusual. Water from shallow wells was highly polluted by open cesspits and the lack of even a rudimentary drainage system in Faversham.

This local demand was met by local supply and from the figures available the barrelages of the local producers can be estimated. Some assumptions have to be made. As there is no evidence of ale brewing by the brewers or in the homes listed in the inventories, the assumption is that ale was brewed, if at all, only in the poorer homes. The % of homes with domestic brewing equipment in the probate inventories is assumed for all homes, for dearth of any other data. The % of brewers market share is based on their individual Brewers Fine expressed as a % of the total of Brewers Fines levied annually by Faversham Corporation of £4. Households brewing at home did not buy any beer. This is a 'working 'model' which aims to provide 'shape' to the Faversham brewing sector between 1650 and 1725.

In the 1660s 64% of homes brewed (based on the probate inventories) which left 36% of demand, or 7,200 barrels per year, to be produced by the common and victualler brewers. Thomas Baldock held between 38% and 57% of this market (based on Brewers Fines) which suggests that his output ranged between 2,700 and 4,100 barrels per year. The victualler brewers produced between 55% and 35% which suggests an output ranging between 3,900 and 2,500 barrels per year, divided between 10 producers. As there is no evidence that common or victualler brewers produced ale, this was beer production.

In the 1670s 50% of homes brewed which left 50% of demand, or 9,500 barrels per year, to be produced by common and victualler brewers. In 1672 James Baldock held 50% of this market which suggests that his output was around 4,750 barrels per year. In 1678 Richard Marsh held 40% of this market which suggests his output was around 3,800 barrels per year. The balance was produced by smaller brewers and the victualler brewers. The Baldock estimate is consistent with the 540 barrels, or a little over 1 months supply, of beer listed in his yard at the time of his death.[309]

By the 1690s 23% of homes brewed which left 77% of demand, or 14,600 barrels per year to be produced by common and victualler brewers. Only 20% was produced by the 6 victualler brewers and 1 small common brewer, so the balance was produced by Richard Marsh and Alexander Bax. Richard Marsh produced 55% or around 8,000 barrels and Alexander Bax produced 25% or around 3,600 barrels per year. In 1699 Richard Marsh held 60% of the market which suggests his peak of annual production at around 8,700 barrels.

In the first decade of the eighteenth century the death of Bax in 1701 and the meteoric rise of Thomas Higgs until his death in 1707 must have skewed local production. The analysis of the probate inventories, the sole source of information at this time,[310] shows that Higgs was larger than Baldock who in turn was smaller than Marsh. It was likely that Higgs would have taken more trade from the Bax Brewery, weakened by the uncertainties of deaths, minorities, trustees and a tenancy holding, than from Marsh. For those 6 years Marsh and Higgs probably held 40% each of market production, Edward Weller, keeping the Bax Brewery running, possibly lost half his trade and the remaining 8% was held by small brewers and victualler brewers. As 15% of homes brewed that left 85% of local demand or 17,000 barrels to be shared by the 3 common brewers. Marsh and Higgs probably brewed around 6,800 barrels each and Weller around 1,700 barrels per year.

By the 1720s home brewing and victualler brewing had contracted further, so around 80% of demand or 17,600 barrels per year would have been produced entirely by Richard Marsh and Edward Weller. If Marsh had recovered his 60% market share his output would have been about 10,000 barrels per year. That of Waller would have been 7,000 barrels per year. This is a range of reasonable probabilities, but alas no solid references have survived to prove them. However, these were very modest amounts. Compared to the output of London breweries, of nearly 2 million barrels per year by 1727, they were insignificant.

This rising output had to be matched by an increasing production of the raw materials of malt and hops. Assuming that the amount used of both per barrel was similar to the previous years, increasing acreages had to be cultivated. Whilst the sources of sufficient barley and malt can be identified the source of sufficient hops is still difficult to identify, at least before the 1720s. Two nagging questions remain; was the beer much weaker than assumed or was less beer produced to bring the volumes brewed more into line with estimated hop production?

In the late seventeenth century barley was being grown both within Faversham and in the surrounding villages. For example, in 1661, Mildmay Maplisden, the brewer and tenant of the Hiltons, had 38 acres of barley growing in the Kingsfield.[311] He was growing his own barley for malting in his own malt house for his own brewery. In 1677 George Sondes, the local territorial magnate but an active farmer, was growing barley on all his main local farms. In Faversham at Homestall Farm he had 66 acres and at Abbey Farm he had 70 acres. Further out he had 60 acres at Lees Court, Sheldwich, 39 acres at Leaveland and 40 acres at Valley Farm, Throwley. He also had a malt house and malt at his Parsonage Farm at Eastry.[312] He was probably growing barley both to sell and to malt himself.

There is no doubt that the Faversham area was growing enough barley to satisfy local demand for malting, and hence brewing, and a considerable surplus of barley and malt for shipping out along the coast, mostly to London. Between 1650 and 1741 the balance of outwards trade of the two reversed. In 1649/50, 210 quarters of barley but 8400 quarters of malt went out.[313] In 1699/1700, 770 quarters of barley but 6180 quarters of malt went out. In 1741, 179 quarters of malt but 2630 quarters of barley went out. In the 5 months from November 1734-March 1735, Faversham sent only 82 quarters of malt but 2664 quarters of barley to London.[314] To put the trade into perspective, 2,500 quarters of malt were needed to produce 15,000 barrels of strong beer. Surpluses for outwards trade were clearly substantial.

At the same time as the volume of malting contracted in Faversham, the common brewers malted barley themselves. In 1667 Thomas Baldock had a malt house in Court Street, James Baldock had a large quantity of malt in an outhouse and in 1702 Alexander Bax had a malt house in his brewery in Preston Street.[315] Richard Marsh had a malt house and contents which were insured as early as 1717 by The Sun Fire Office[316] and Edward Weller also insured his malt house, at the White Hart, 22 Court Street, from 1719.[317]

Further down the scale, most victualler brewers depended on the local maltsters for their supplies. Thomas Higgs was the exception with a malt house, probably at the Standard.[318] The others were too small to support an independent malt house.[319]

The source of hops is not so easy to follow. Approximately 100 acres of hops were needed to produce 15,000 barrels of strong beer or 60 acres of hops to produce small beer.[320] Compared to the thousands of acres in the villages surrounding Faversham a few acres of hop gardens are insignificant. That explains why references to them are scant. Research suggests that the hop gardens were very small,[321] often moved but were on most farms, until the eighteenth century. The problem of identification is compounded by the absence of references to hops in most probate inventories; listing of them, whether in the ground or in the house was not required. Hop growing was deemed akin to gardening.

In the 1690s Celia Fiennes refers to the hop gardens scattered along the Sittingbourne to Faversham Road and in the 1720s Daniel Defoe refers to the great increase in hop gardens around Canterbury. In the first half of the eighteenth century evidence of hop gardens around Faversham emerges. They were on the rich brick earths of the Kingsfield, Cooksditch Farm, and Preston Farm. By 1725 Vincent Williams and Mr Gruber[322] had hop gardens in Kingsfield,[323] Henry Best had hop gardens in Gallowshole Field, Thomas Amis had a hop garden in Cuthorne and Dr Everard had hop gardens nearby. By 1732 William Pepper of Mall House had hop gardens in the Pound Ground,[324] Robert Rade, Mr Gibbs, Dr Everard and Mr Gruber all had oast houses in the town. At Cooksditch Farm the Smiths had hop gardens by 1731.[325] Further south on Preston Farm[326] in the 1730s Mr Budds, a Faversham maltster, had 2 acres of hops; Mr Clements had 1 acre; Mr Gibbs, Mr Walker and Mr Ovenden had 2 1/2 acres of hops; Mr Carter had 1 1/2 acres; Mr Ovenden had 2 acres; and Mr Pepper and Mr Plane had 2 acres. Those 10 acres would have been sufficient to produce 1,500 barrels of strong beer.

By 1745 there was no doubt about the local source of hops; Faversham was surrounded by hop gardens.[327] [Plan 5]. They stretched from Lower Road and South Road to Whitstable Road, east to near Love Lane and south to the London Road. At least 60 acres were grown north of the London Road and more must have been planted south. This was enough to produce nearly 10,000 barrels of beer. In the 1740s and 1750s Samuel Shepherd, the successor to Richard Marsh at The Brewery, had 7 acres of hop gardens at Preston Farm.[328] In 1732 an Edward Rigden of Canterbury also had a 1 acre hop garden.[329] Brewers were concerned about protecting supplies of their primary ingredient.

Whilst the size of the earlier hop gardens cannot be quantified, they did produce surpluses, at least in some years, to local demand. Identifiable quantities were sent up to London by sea but there is no way of calculating what was transported by road over short distances. For example in 1656 20 bags of hops were sent up. Of these 13 bags, together with quantities of malt and gunpowder, were despatched by Daniel Judd of Syndale, the Parliamentarian gunpowder manufacturer of Faversham; just the sort of entrepreneur one would expect to be experimenting with hops and malting. In 1663 36 bags went up; some from John Knowler, the Castlocke grandson. In 1688 176 bags were sent up and in 1692 87 bags went up. 1699/1700 must have been an extraordinary year, either of yields or a temporary use of Faversham port, as 1700 bags were despatched. In the 9 months recorded in 1741 2680 bags were sent from Faversham by sea to London.[330] Here was a local industry which had taken off.

Once this industry achieved a critical size it spawned new trade titles of hop planter and hop merchant for its dedicated participants. By 1738 Vincent Williams of Faversham was described as a hop planter, with 'oasts and stowages' in Preston. By 1737 John Waller of Faversham was described as a hop merchant with stock and warehouses at One and Two Pair of Stairs, Southwark, insured for £500.[331] His grand-daughter married Henry Shepherd junior, a later partner in The Brewery. In Canterbury, also surrounded by hop gardens, there was a similar development. These titles were not used there either before 1700. Between 1700 and 1725 7 hop planter Freemen of Canterbury are known and between 1725 and 1750 10 hop planter Freemen of Canterbury are known. Only between 1725 and 1750 are 2 hop merchants known as Freemen of Canterbury.[332] By the early eighteenth century Canterbury, it would appear, had become a much larger centre of hop growing than Faversham.

The distribution or sales outlets for beer changed little during this period; there was direct trade, tied trade and free trade. All brewers had a substantial private trade, direct from producer to consumer, which continued well into the nineteenth century. Distribution through public houses varied. The victualler brewers, such a feature of the period, had their own in-house tied trade. The Common brewers probably sold to all public houses and only at the very end of the period did they have a sustained tied house trade. Even then that part of their trade was small.

In 1662 Faversham had 30 licensed victuallers.[333] [Tables 7 & 8]. In 1691 there were 31 licensed victuallers. In 1710 the numbers had fallen to 24 where they remained in 1731. The concentration of these continued to be in the centre of the town and the newcomers operated at the edges, especially near the Creek. Houses with romantic names like the Bostsun and Call, the Zurrickzee and the Kings Head at the Key had short lives. The long established houses like the Ship, the Bear and the Fleur de Lys remained. The arrival of newcomers probably had little to do with population changes but more to do with the embanking of the Creek and water born trade.

Ownership of most public houses was separate from operation. The better houses were owned by substantial merchants, with only tenuous connections to brewing through the malt trade. In 1680 for example the Swann was owned by Mark Trowtes; the Horne was owned by Boys Owre; and the Crowne by William Watson. The Queens Arms was owned by the Town.[334] By 1717 ownerships had changed to a more diverse range of occupations. With the exception of the Dolphin, which was owned by Peter Grenstreet, one of the local farming family, and the two Marsh and the two Bax houses, the owners of the others had no immediate connections with the brewing industry.[335]

The exception was the Ship. By 1660 it was owned by the heirs of William Dix, the common brewer who for a time ran the Castlocke Brewery. By 1672 it was owned by James Baldock, who took over The Brewery, and was occupied by Widow Barker. In 1680 it was still owned by his heirs. By 1691 until his death in 1706 it was owned and occupied by Thomas Higgs, the great victualler brewer, who also owned the Three Tuns in Tanners Street. James Baldock owned one other public house in Faversham, the Cherry Tree, at 10/11 Preston Street, which was occupied by Edward Knowler. The leading Common Brewer of his day owned the leading inn of his day and the leading Victualler Brewer then owned the leading inn of his day. At the time they were novel and foresighted developments and no doubt profitable.

The potential of these developments was not lost on others. Richard Marsh, Baldock's successor, probably because he did not have free capital to do so, never bought a central public house. He did buy the Castle, at 76 West Street in 1711 and the Three Tuns, in Tanners Street, in 1715.[336] They were small operations on the fringe of Faversham but which had no other public houses. The

Castle was possibly converted into a public house by Marsh. The Three Tuns, which had been at 22 West Street, was closed and the licence relocated by Thomas Higgs to the new site in Tanners Street. The Three Tuns in particular would have catered for the leather workers in Tanners Street and both for the gunpowder workers at the Home Gunpowder Works. This nascent tied estate was expanded steadily by the Marsh successor, Samuel Shepherd, later in the century.[337]

Alexander Bax also started a tied estate in the 1690s, which in turn was developed by the Rigden Brewery successors. At the time of his death he had acquired the Masons Arms at 13 Preston Street and the George by then at 50 Preston Street. One was out of the town centre but the other was the first public house on the way into the town from the south east. Both were modest tenanted houses.

With the exception of Thomas Higgs none of the victualler brewers owned their houses. They were tenants, with all the uncertainties that brought for investment in plant and equipment. This may explain why they were modest operators and a short lived phenomenon.

The supply relationships of common brewers to publicans is not easy to determine. The slender evidence shows that two independent victuallers owed brewers money. Thomas May who died in 1682, owed £35.10.0 to 'Mr Marsh the Brewer'[338] and Edward Knowler who died in 1679 owed James Baldock £50 for beer.[339] This equates to about 70 barrels of strong beer. The 4 other publicans, for whom accounts survive, who were all victualler brewers, had no debts for beer to any brewers but they did have related debts. Thomas Borsley in 1671 owed Mr Rigden for malt; Richard Foster at the Ship in 1673 owed Amy Baldock for malt, tobacco and pipes; John Fryer in 1673 owed money for malt; and Arthur Whitlocke had no such debts.[340] Two other examples of an association of common brewers with independent victuallers survive. In 1673 the probate inventory of Edward Thorogood, at the Bell in Preston Street, was drawn up by James Baldock;[341] and in 1697 the probate inventory of Richard Willis was signed by Richard Marsh.[342] In 1689 the probate inventory of William Varham, victualler brewer at the Bear, was drawn up by Thomas Hilton, maltster. These few examples suggest that independent houses were supplied by common Brewers but victualler brewers were not.

The relationships of victuallers to victuallers is easier to follow. The vast majority of guarantees or Recognisances [Table 8] of publicans were other publicans. No common brewer guaranteed a publican. In 1691 65% of the recognisances were given by victuallers and by 1710 80% of the recognisances were given by victuallers. The few victualler brewers giving guarantees appear to have given them only to the smallest houses; and Thomas Higgs gave none. This suggests that victualler brewers produced enough for their own trade and did not supply other houses. The publicans who did not brew were happy to guarantee their rivals and in 1710 Mathew Denham of the Bear and Thomas Varham of the Turks Head, 4 Court Street, especially so. One wonders what advantage it was for them.

Trade at a leading inn, such as the Ship, was substantial, for not only did it cater for local trade, but it catered for a wide range of travellers. The Ship maintained a range of rooms which were named.[343] In 1673 there was the Parlour, the Great Parlour, the Stag and Greyhound, the Sun Chamber, the Three Tuns Chamber, the Boardseyed Chamber, the Bell Chamber, the Star Chamber and the Great Chamber over the Parlour. Below stairs were cellars containing two pipes of canary wine, 4 hogsheads of claret, 2 hogsheads of white wine and 68 barrels of strong beer. Outside there was stabling and at the end of the sign was a garland or bush.

Not all trade was welcome. At a time when there were few barracks or hospitals to accommodate the armed forces the only alternative accommodation was at inns and private houses. The importance of this is shown by the lists kept by the Lords Lieutenant of the numbers of beds and stables available.[344] Accepting billeting by the state was obligatory. Faversham, being a port and close to the Continent, always suffered. During the Second Dutch War Faversham had to take in 505 sick or wounded seamen between October 1665 and January 1667.[345] 80 households took in these men for an average stay of 40 days. Faversham victuallers bore the brunt. For example, John Clare at the Crowne had to accommodate 19 men; Henry Leese at the Dolphin took in 18 men; Nicholas Bennett took in 17; and Widow Baker took in 31.

The profit from the additional demand for 400 barrels of small beer and the total additional income of £1000 for Faversham during the Second Dutch War was probably marginal. The payment by the state of 1/- per day per man billeted was no compensation for lice, disease and disorder brought to an inn. Moreover, for a government always short of revenue, payment of victuallers in full was uncertain. At the time of his death in 1673 Richard Foster at the Ship[346] held £17.13.0 of 'Tickets for Soldiers Billeted'. One wonders how long these had been outstanding and how often they had been discounted.

One other result of war was the shortage of small coin and the issuing of tokens by townsmen. These low value coins, for a farthing or a half penny, appeared in the 1650s but most were produced in the 1660s.[347] 14 different coins are known to have been produced in Faversham; 52 in Canterbury; 48 in Dover; 20 in Maidstone; and 19 in Sandwich. Many were produced by victuallers and grocers. In Faversham 4 were produced by victuallers. In 1651 R.E.C. minted a 1/4d; in 1664 Robert Preston of the Queens Arms minted a 1/2d; in 1666 John Cleare of the Crowne minted a 1/2d; and about 1663 Robert Hogben at the Three Tuns produced a 1/2d. A good supply of small change appears to have been most needed by the victuallers and especially those with seamen billeted upon them.

In addition to the regular sales of beer there were always occasional direct sales of beer by the brewers. The Corporation continued to buy small amounts of beer for special events. Celebrations, visits and dinners all needed alcohol. The Faversham Workhouse was a more regular source of direct sales. In 1724, for example, the Overseers of the Poor paid both Richard Marsh and Mr Weller for beer delivered.[348] Marsh received £8.6.0 and Weller received £6.0.0. Assuming this was for Small Beer and not Strong Beer approximately 35 barrels of beer were sold.

Regulation of the brewing industry remained in place. Faversham Corporation still appointed ale conners to test brews and bring miscreants to a local court. The only beers produced continued to be strong beer and small beer. At the national level the introduction of the Excise Tax in 1656 gradually brought more supervision of the industry, not least to check under reporting. Victuallers were licensed each year by Faversham Corporation.

Competition to the brewers product, wine, continued. In 1662 Mrs Elizabeth Davies was retailing wine 'and by virtue of the Statute she must appear before the Commissioners in London. Captain Trowtes will appear upon her behalf'. By 1665 Mr Robert Preston and Mrs Anne Baker had licences to retail wine. In the 1670s the Baldocks had Wine Licences. Robert Platt at the Queens Arms had one by at least 1672 and Richard Foster and Thomas Higgs both had Wine Licences at the Ship.[349]

One modest new competitor to beer drinking in Faversham was coffee. By 1718 4 Court Street was described as a Coffee House. The owners were John and Henry Rigden, possibly related to the brewers, and the occupier was Thomas Varham.[350] Not only did he serve the new drink but he had a victuallers licence and he was the town's Post Master.[351] As the term coffee house does not reappear coffee drinking probably became common, especially at home, and the activity outside the home was common in better quality inns.

The public lives of the common brewers followed those of their predecessors. They continued to take an active part in local affairs as commoners, jurats and occasionally mayors. Climbing the Corporation ladder took time. Richard Marsh senior was mayor in 1708, 30 years after his arrival in Faversham but his son Richard Marsh junior became mayor in 1722 and 1725. Alexander Bax never became mayor, but his gentleman son, Stephen, became mayor in 1720. Edward Weller was mayor in 1714 and 1727. The only victualler brewer and innkeeper to become mayor was Thomas Higgs in 1702, only 12 years after his arrival in Faversham; another example of him being an exceptional man.[352] Further down the scale, none of the other victualler brewers or publicans became mayors or jurats; comment as much upon their economic status as their trade.

A public office that both Richard Marsh senior and Edward Weller, who succeeded him, held was Captain of the Trained Bands of Faversham. There was a military hierarchy and they were answerable to the Lords Lieutenant of Kent. This local militia of able men between the ages of 16 and 60 assembled annually to drill with arms and to remain ready for any emergency. At times of national emergency, when there was no standing army, these were highly responsible positions. In December 1688 Richard Marsh was put to the test when for a few days Faversham became the centre of national politics and security.

The flight of James II from London and his capture by fishermen who brought him to Faversham must have brought alarm to the town. Here was a figure who provoked strong feelings for and against Roman Catholics, not least because the town's Charter had been revoked and replaced recently by his government. Mobs could form quickly, the Roman Catholic Sir Edward Hales lived locally at Tunstall, the ambivalent Lewis Duras, 2nd Earl of Faversham, owned much property around the town and detachments of Horse Guards and Grenadiers were sent from London to secure the King. Within two days the King was gone and the Trained Bands were not called out. Marsh, who was with the King for much of the time, and was the first to recognise him, clearly acted competently to help to avoid a confrontation which could quickly lead to rioting and the destruction of property.[353] What the King did leave with Marsh in Faversham was a small sheet of paper listing the verses in the Bible setting out the duties of subjects to a monarch.[354]

Richard Marsh was faced again in 1715 by national events affecting Faversham. The successful rising in Scotland of the son of James II, The Old Pretender, and his advance as far as Derby again provoked fury against Roman Catholics locally. Nash Court at Boughton, the home of the Hawkins family, and only two miles from Faversham, was sacked by a Protestant mob. Had drunken mob rule spilled over the importance of the Captain of Trained Bands to maintain order would again have been tested. Captain Edward Weller never had to confront such events.

Richard Marsh senior was not the only member of his family to be involved in the defence of Kent. His nephew, Thomas Marsh, the son of his eldest brother Henry, was by 1688 Captain of the Trained Bands of Dover and by 1696 he was Deputy Lieutenant of Dover Castle. He was a Lieutenant Colonel of the Cinque Ports Militia, the Captain of Sandown Castle and subsequently a Deputy Lieutenant of Kent and Justice of the Peace.[355] As a medium sized landowner, he was a typical member of the administration of the county.[356]

The private lives of these men are difficult to discover for none of their papers have survived. For most of the Marsh family Nethersole House and Womenswold, near Deal, where many of them were buried, was considered home. Neither Richard senior or junior established a new lasting branch of the family in Faversham, but those children who did survive were successful. Richard senior had three sons, [Marsh Pedigree], upon whom he settled the largest part of his estate during his lifetime.[357]

The eldest son, John, was educated at Pembroke College, Cambridge, and was admitted as a barrister at Middle Temple in 1706 aged 21. He was appointed Treasurer in 1747. By the time he died, a childless widower, in 1752 under his will[358] he left at least £15,000 plus the Nethersole estate at Womenswold, which produced £1,000 to £1,500 per annum in rent.[359] He left also an important library, to remain as an heirloom at Nethersole House, and, amongst other things, a Thomas Tompion watch.[360] There were specific bequests to maternal cousins, General and Colonel Sabine, to Marsh relations and to a staff of coachmen, cook, housekeeper and servants. He left money to the poor of Womenswold and Kingston in Kent and £2,000 to the Company of Faversham Oyster Dredgermen. To the surprise of his contemporaries he left the income from the estate to his friend, the surgeon John Winchester of Norfolk Street, for his life. Thereafter it reverted to the grandson of his first cousin, Henry Marsh.[361] Under his father's will John received in 1726 the real estate in Ash, Romney Marsh and Lydd and the remaining personal estate. He was commemorated by his friend with a fine monument in Womenswold Church surmounted by a bust;[362] the only known surviving portrait of a Marsh.

The second son, Richard Marsh junior, spent his entire life in Faversham. He had probably taken over The Brewery by 1710 when his father had retired to Womenswold. Richard married Mary Bax, the daughter of Alexander Bax the competitor brewer. They had two children; Anne who died in infancy and Silvester who died unmarried aged 24 and who is commemorated by a wall monument in the chancel of the Faversham Parish Church. Richard died intestate aged 40,[363] only a year after his father. It is unlikely that his estate comprised more than The Brewery, the Three Tuns and the Castle public houses, a leased malt house and a few thousand pounds of stock. His total estate was probably worth no more than £4,000. Brewing in the provinces was not an immediate route to ever increasing wealth. His wife would have received a lifetime income from this but Silvester would have been the main beneficiary, albeit held temporarily in trust. It is interesting to speculate if she were trained as a teenager in the business she would ultimately inherit, but which during her minority was run by her mother and her stepfathers, Hilles Hobday and then Samuel Shepherd.[364] Richard was buried at Womenswold. Alas, the character of Richard Marsh junior barely emerges beyond someone who just kept the business he inherited running.

The youngest son, Henry, appears to have spent his life away from Faversham. Whilst he married twice and his three children were baptised then buried as infants there, he is not listed as a Faversham resident.[365] One glimpse of his life has emerged. On 23 January 1713 his brother, Richard Marsh, wrote him a letter in which he is described as a merchant at Boston, New England. It concerns the shipwreck of his sailors. The letter was never sent but survived in the archives of the Portsmouth Overseers.[366] Henry was mentioned in his father's will dated 1718 as having had property settled on him at the time of his marriage. His date and place of death are unknown.

Perhaps he was the classic adventurous youngest son who went to the developing colonies to seek fame and fortune, but simply disappeared.

The premature death of Richard Marsh junior leaving a young wife and a young daughter in 1727 once again threatened the continuation of the brewery. Were it not for the ability and determination of his widow, Mary Marsh, the business could easily have collapsed or passed again out of the family. It was probably due to the upbringing of Mary, the daughter of that other self made Faversham brewer Alexander Bax, which saved it. She must have been steeped in the practice of brewing from childhood and throughout her marriage.

Mary ran the business for a year and in 1728 married a Canterbury widower, Hilles Hobday, who moved to Faversham. In 1731 she was widowed again and by the end of that year she married for a third time, Samuel Shepherd. As neither husband is recorded as a brewer it is likely that Mary remained active in the business for some time into the 1730s not least to protect the interests of her daughter, Silvester Marsh. From that responsibility she was relieved by the early death of Silvester, unmarried, aged 24 in 1743. The brewery passed almost seamlessly to the Shepherd family.[367]

## CHAPTER SIX

# Conclusion

The emergence let alone the survival of one business in a small town over many centuries was remarkable. The reasons were clearly varied but over time there were a number of common threads which help to explain why this business took root and continues in the twenty-first century as 'Britain's Oldest Brewer.' Here was a collection of interacting market, family and human factors. The pathway of development from the sixteenth century to the early eighteenth century, and then down to today, was like a mass of crazy paving which was cemented in unevenly and haphazardly over time.

Until supplies of purified water from the newly established Faversham Water Company were available from the 1860s and the consumption of tea and coffee became widespread, beer was a basic necessity of life. Early brewers did not have to cultivate a market place, that from the 1860s became one for an increasingly recreational product. Population growth brought automatic growth to the sector. Only when the product was shifting to becoming a recreational one was there a scramble by breweries to buy and tie public houses. Provided brewers produced a good product at a reasonable price they would survive.

The choice of the site of The Brewery at 18 Court Street Faversham was not by chance. Here was a supply of unlimited water from an artesian well, which bubbled up naturally from the ground. A well did not have to be sunk nor water pumped up. This was recognised by at least 1573 and possibly close by in Partridge Lane, on what is now part of The Brewery site, by 1507. None of the other brewers had this advantage.

Businesses before the passing of the Companies Acts in the mid nineteenth century were family concerns. Provided there were heirs the business survived. If not the business either collapsed or went through a period of uncertainty and all that meant for holding customers. Assets could not be transferred, and hence the business protected, through shares.

The Castlocke family had a succession of four generations of male heirs who lived to take over the Brewery. When that family became extinct there were some years of uncertainty then revival under another family, the Baldocks. The pattern was repeated and then the business was revived again under the Marsh family.

This situation was not unique to those families. The Hiltons had a succession of male heirs but then disappeared from brewing in the 1650s as a result of a minority. Alexander Bax had a son who took on the business for a time. In the sixteenth century the Stransham family had a profusion of male heirs, William Tomlin had at least a profusion of female heirs, and in 1707 Thomas Higgs had three daughters, but that was not enough to retain the business.

The vital factor which tempered all family successions was the human factor of commitment to the business and the will to succeed. Without those however successful the business or however good the succession planning the family business would fade away or pass to new owners.

The Stransham and the Bax families established good breweries but their children retired from the businesses to become leisured gentlemen. The first generation of Castlocke, Baldock and Marsh were all younger sons who showed entrepreneurial drive to establish themselves in a new sector and their descendants showed the will to continue the business they inherited.

Hopefully these pages go some way to separating myth from fact and to answering the two most often asked questions of Shepherd Neame: how old are you and why have you survived.

# Footnotes

## Chapter One

1. Valerie Fenwick. Recent Work on the Graveney Boat. National Maritime Museum. Maritime Monographs and Reports. 1972. p.16.
2. Information from Michael Frohnsdorff and Jack Long. See under for taxation dates.
3. Calendar of Patent Rolls. 1311 Volume. p.322.
4. Faversham Borough Archives. Kent History and Library Centre. (KHLC). Ref. Fa/RTz 2/1 & 2. A Tallage was a manorial tax levied on Faversham by the Abbot, as Lord of the Manor of Faversham. The Manor of Faversham covered the whole of the town, with the exception of a few properties in Preston Street, Market Place and West Street. The Abbey site and Abbey Farm were not included. The survival of the main Tallage suggests that it was both comprehensive and used as a precedent in later years. For a full transcript of the lists see Hyde & Harrington, The Early Town Books of Faversham pp. 542-546.
5. Historians have assumed that the population of England after the Black Death did not recover previous levels until the late sixteenth century.
6. Note from Jack Long quoting from Food in Mediaeval England (Diet and Nutrition). OUP. Mediaeval History and Archaeology series.
7. See below for the tax details.
8. Note from J. Long.
9. Ed. P. Tann. Edward Crow. Notes.
10. Note from J. Long . Op. Cit.
11. J. Bennett. Ale, Beer and Brewsters in England. Women's Work in a Changing World. p.31.
12. P. Clark & L. Murfit. The History of Maidstone. p.30.
13. Note provided by Michael Frohnsdorff.
14. M. Frohnsdorff in P. Tann. Royal Charters of Faversham. pp.55 & 61.
15. P. Tann. Op .Cit. p.62.
16. D. Wright translations in P. Tann. Op. Cit. p.107.
17. Note provided by Jack Long.
18. E. Jacob. History of Faversham.
19. Clark & Murfit. Op. Cit. p.30.
20. Poole. Domesday Book to Magna Carta. p.58. Note provided by Michael Frohnsdorff.
21. Note provided by J. Long and M. Frohnsdorff.
22. Calendar of Patent Rolls. 1311. p.322.
23. J. Bennett. Op. Cit. p.17.
24. Note from J. Long quoting from B.F. Harvey. Monastic Pittances.
25. Kent Archaeological Society. Archbishop Peckham's Survey of Kent Manors 1283/1285. pp. 175, 198, 141/4 and 155.

## Chapter Two

26. Faversham Borough Archives. KHLC. Ref. FaZ3. Archaeologia Cantiana. Vol VII. Cades Rebellion and Kent. p.265.
27. Faversham Abbey Leiger Book. Rockingham Castle Archives. Copy in the author's library. I am very grateful to Duncan Harrington for pointing out this reference.
28. J. M. Cowper. Canterbury Freeman Lists.
29. Faversham Abbey Leiger Book. Op.Cit. p.69.
30. Faversham Manor Rentals. KHLC. Refs. U390. M.
31. J. Owen. The Court Rolls and Rentals of the Manor of Davington.
32. Will. KHLC. Ref: PRC17/2/461.
33. K. Jacob. Faversham Biographical Register.
34. K. Jacob. Op. Cit.
35. R. A. Pelham. Sussex Trade. Sussex Archaeological Collections. Vol. 71. pp.186-188.
36. J. Bennet. Op. Cit. p.80.
37. The National Archives.(NA). Ref: E179/230/200C.
38. Clarke, Pearson, Mate and Parfitt. Sandwich to 1600. p.140.
39. Calendar of Patent Rolls. 1436-1441. p.495.

40. M. Mate. Trade and Economic Development. Kent Surrey and Sussex. pp.16 & 63.
41. M. Mate. Op. Cit. p.140.
42. M. Mate. Op. Cit. p.16.
43. Bennett. Op. Cit. p.85.
44. L. F. Salzman. English Trade in the Middle Ages. p.360.
45. Ed. H. Bradley. The Views of the Hosts of Alien Merchants, 1440-1444. pp.4 & 84.
46. R. Scott. The Perfect Platform for a Hop Garden. 1576.
47. KHCL. Ref. PRC 17/5 f.73.
48. KHCL. Ref. PRC 17/9 f.224.
49. Calendar of Patent Rolls. 19 Henry VI Part 1. p.495.
50. P. Hyde & D. Harrington. Early Town Books of Faversham. pp.48, 81, 85, 548.

## Chapter Three

51. This Table has been compiled from a range of sources noted in Table 2.
52. For the years 1547-1551 the Brewers Fines listed in The Faversham Wardmote Books verify these numbers.
53. Rev. G Streynsham Master. Family of Streynsham. pp.7-9.
54. W. Telfer. Faversham's Last Abbott. Faversham Papers 1. p.6.
55. P. Hyde & D. Harrington. Thomas Arden, The Man and the Myth. p.396.
56. Letters and Papers of Henry VIII. Volume 15. 14 January 1540/1541.
57. Telfer. Op. Cit. p.7. Glover was a lay butler at the Abbey.
58. Telfer. Op. Cit. pp.12, 14.
59. Administration. KHCL. Ref. PRC3/9 f.43.
60. Freemen of Canterbury. Op. Cit. p.290.
61. KHCL. Ref. PRC3/12 f.52.
62. No will or administration of his estate has been found.
63. P. Hyde & D.Harrington. Faversham Muster Rolls. p.10. Ref. KHLC Fa CPm 1 onwards.
64. Archdeaconry Court Register. Canterbury Cathedral Archive.(CCA). Ref: PRC 39/10 f.49.
65. Faversham Muster Rolls. Op. Cit.
66. Arden. Op. Cit. pp. 385, 404.
67. NA. Refs. C 131/101/8 & 23.
68. Family of Streynsham. Op. Cit. p.12.
69. Arden. Op. Cit. See references to 1532 Rental and premises 'late Laurence Stransham'.
70. Faversham Town Books. Op. Cit. p.133.
71. Will. KHLC. Ref. PRC17/42 f.305.
72. Faversham Town Books. Op. Cit. Index.
73. Will. NA. Ref. PROB11/104 f.229.
74. Will. NA. Ref. PROB11/66 f.116.
75. Kent Visitation of Arms. 1594. The grant was made by Robert Cooke, Clarenceux Herald.
76. Up to 1559 there are no Faversham Cole wills in the Archdeaconry Court Registers.
77. Faversham Town Books. Op. Cit. pp.266, 270.
78. Faversham Muster Rolls. Op. Cit.
79. Will. KHLC. Ref. PRC17/50 f.238.
80. Will. KHLC. Ref. PRC17/63 f. 244
81. Davington Manor Rentals. Op.Cit. 2/6 Preston Street.
82. Faversham Fines. Kent Archaeological Website. Duncan Harrington. KHLC. Ref. FaJBf.1-36.
83. Faversham Muster Rolls. Op. Cit.
84. Town Books. Op. Cit. p.540.
85. Faversham Abbey Leiger Book. Op. Cit. f.197.
86. Faversham Town Books. Op. Cit. p.104.
87. Faversham Town Books. Op. Cit. p.121.
88. Faversham Muster Rolls. Op. Cit.
89. Faversham Muster Rolls. Op. Cit.
90. Faversham Parish Church Registers.CCA. Bishops Transcripts.
91. Faversham Muster Rolls. Op. Cit.
92. Faversham Parish Church Registers. CCA. Bishops Transcripts.
93. Calendar of Patent Rolls. 4 & 5 Philip and Mary. p.285.
94. Watson Rockingham Castle Archives. Ref. MSS 681.
95. Telfer. Op. Cit. p.14.
96. Letters and Papers of Henry VIII. Vol. 15. 14 Jan. 1540/1541.
97. Arden. Op. Cit. Abbey Rental. 1532. pp.426/429.
98. Edward Crow. Notes. Op.Cit. p.435.
99. Faversham Muster Rolls. Op. Cit.
100. Faversham Abbey Leiger Book. Op. Cit. p.69.
101. Faversham Abbey Leiger Book. Op. Cit. f.197v.
102. Faversham Muster Rolls. Op. Cit.
103. Will. KHLC. Ref. PRC 17/50 f.238.
104. Faversham Parish Registers. Bishops Transcripts. CCA.
105. Bargain Sale and Feoffment . 24 February 1610/11. National Archives. Ref. E44.263. Faversham Fines. 21 January 2 James I and 15 January 5 James I. KHLC. Ref. Fa JBf. 1-36. Kent Archaeological Society Web Site. Faversham Fines. Transcribed by D. Harrington. Will. KHLC. Ref. PRC 17/63 f.244.
106. Davington Manor Rentals. Op. Cit.
107. Faversham Muster Rolls. Op. Cit.
108. Faversham Muster Rolls. Op.Cit. 1570 to 1600.
109. When he died in 1593 his children were all minors which suggests that he was born about 1555.
110. Will. KHLC. PRC 17/42 f.305.
111. Will. NA. PROB 11/66 f.15.
112. P. Mathias. History of Brewing. Table 37. p.542.
113. See below for references.
114. Probate Inventories. Archdeaconry Court. 1565-1800. KHCL. Refs. PRC10 and PRC11. See also typed List of Inventories. 1565-1587. KHCL. Refs. PRC10/1-16.
115. The values are shown in pre-decimalised English currency, which was introduced in 1970. In old currency £1 =20 shillings (s). 1 shilling=12 old pence (d). In new decimalised currency £1=100 new pence (p). 1 shilling=5 new pence. 1 old penny=0.42 new pence.
116. Arden. Op. Cit. p.458.
117. Ref. Probate Inventories. Op. Cit.
118. Sandwich Customs Book. 35/36 Henry VIII, 1543/1544. NA. Ref. E122 130/15. Transcribed in Arden. pp.164-179. Op. Cit. London Port Book. 1567. NA Ref. E190 4/2 Faversham Port Books. Overseas and Coastal In and Out (Incomplete before 1587). 1570 onwards. NA. Ref. E190/588 onwards. As the Customs Port of Faversham included the ports of Whitstable and Herne it is not always easy to allocate trade to the Faversham port. Faversham port was by far the larger. More ships originated there. As The Port Books usually note the home port of the vessels this is used to allocate the trade.

119. NA. Refs. E.190/588 and onwards.
120. As above.
121. Probate Inventory. KHLC. Ref: PRC10/5/29.
122. Faversham Town Books. Op. Cit. p.107.
123. Faversham Town Books. Op. Cit. pp.195 & 230.
124. Faversham Town Books. Op. Cit. pp.242, 267, 307 etc.
125. Faversham Town Books. Op. Cit. pp. 439 & 504.
126. Sandwich Customs Port Books. NA. Ref. E.122/208/3.
127. See footnote 114 above. Op. Cit. Arden.pp.164-179.
128. Arden. Op .Cit. p.164. Footnote 408.
129. Special Supplement to The Brewers Journal. Hop Statistics 1813-1913. May 15 1913. These show acreages, totals grown, imports, exports, estimated consumption and prices by region. P. Mathias. Op. Cit. In 1830, 8.83m barrels of beer were produced.
130. Faversham Port Books. NA. Ref. E190/640/2 & 10.
131. Faversham Port Book. NA. Ref.E190/643/19.
132. Faversham Port Books. NA. Ref. E190/645/3.
133. Faversham port Books. NA. Ref. E190/646/6.
134. See note 121 above. In the 1830s 50,000 acres of hops (average acreage per year for the decade) produced 314,000cwt of hops per annum (average per year for the decade). ie. 1 acre produced about 6 1/4 cwt of hops on average per annum in the 1830s.
135. C. W. Chalklin. Seventeenth Century Kent. p.282 for index to hops.
136. Saxton Map of Homestall Farm. KHLC. Ref. U390. P2.
137. Faversham Port Books. 1543 and 1570 onwards. NA Ref. E190.
138. Faversham Port Books. NA. Ref. E190/646/8.
139. I am grateful to Shepherd Neame brewer Richard Frost for information on the quantity of malt used in production today. Conversion to output 400 years earlier is entirely the authors calculation in an attempt to put the trade of late sixteenth century Faversham into national context.
140. Faversham Town Books. Op. Cit. pp.325, 361, 382, 406, 463.
141. A barrel was 36 or 30 gallons. A kilderkin was half a barrel or 15-18 gallons. A firkin was half a kilderkin or 8-9 gallons.
142. A detailed survey of the surviving Probate Accounts for the period, which list debts, would throw light on this subject. They were all indexed by Peter Spufford for The British Record Society in 1999. The original documents are at KHCL. Ref. PRC2.
143. Faversham Manor Rental. CCA. Ref. Literary MSS B5. See Arden. Op. Cit. p.390.
144. Will. KHLC. Ref. PRC17/5/73.
145. Faversham Recognisances. 1570-1620. KHLC. Refs. Fa/JQr/2.
146. NA. Ref. SP12/16/20. The Hundred of Faversham includes the villages north and south of the town.
147. Will 1570. KHLC. Ref. PRC17/41 f.450.
148. Faversham Manor Rental 1604. KHLC. Ref. U390.M38.
149. Will. 1587. KHLC. PRC17/47 f.123.
150. Faversham Leiger Book. Op. Cit. f.197. Arden . Op. Cit. p.435.
151. Faversham Manor Rental. Op. Cit.
152. See above.
153. See above. Will.
154. Faversham Manor Rental 1604. Op Cit.
155. Faversham Tipplers Recognisances. Op. Cit.
156. Will. 1589. KHLC. Ref. PRC17/48 f.198. Faversham Muster Lists. Op. Cit.
157. Will. 1592. KHLC. Ref. PRC17/49 f.246.
158. Will. KHLC. Ref. PRC17/42 f.347. Faversham Tipplers Recognisances. Op. Cit.
159. Faversham Manor Rentals. 1604 and 1608. Op. Cit.
160. Will. KHLC. Ref. PRC17/17 f.314.
161. Will. KHLC. Ref. PRC17/51 f.280.
162. Faversham Tipplers Recognisances. 1570-1620. Op. Cit.
163. Faversham Town Books. Op. Cit. pp.207, 213 & 253.
164. Faversham Port Books. NA. Ref. E190/643/7.
165. Acts of The Privy Council. HMSO. 1576-7. p.280.
166. Faversham Town Books. Op. Cit. p.177.
167. Faversham Town Books. Op. Cit. p.326.
168. Acts of the Privy Council. 1591. p.188.
169. Acts of the Privy Council. 1600. Vol.31. p.19.
170. If 25% of the population were male and spent only 20% of their time at an ale house and drank twice the day time quantity that equalled 10%.
171. See above.
172. A seed sown with wheat.
173. Faversham Port Books. Op. Cit. E190/648/8.
174. Faversham Town Books. Op. Cit.
175. Faversham Manor Rental. 1604. KHLC. Ref. U390/38.
176. Archaeologia Cantiana. Vol. 2. p.400.
177. Faversham Town Books. Op. Cit.
178. Archaeologia Cantiana. Op. Cit.
179. See following chapter for detail.
180. Faversham Town Books. Op. Cit.
181. Faversham Muster Books. Op. Cit. KHLC. 1573 Ref. FaCPm/3.
182. The Shepherds of Shepherd Neame. 1732-1876. Op. Cit.
183. Data is scarce. No Probate Accounts or Probate Inventories survive at this period for any Faversham brewer. The surviving wills mention some properties and specific money requests. All leave residues which are not quantified. Real estate is often not mentioned.
184. Will. 1593. KHLC. Ref. PRC 17/50 f.238.
185. Will. 1590. KHLC. Ref. PRC 17/48 f.17.
186. The Freemen of Canterbury. Op. Cit.
187. Similar analysis of easily accessible comparable data for Sandwich and Maidstone would confirm the importance of the brewing industry for Faversham.

## Chapter Four

188. Faversham Brewers Fines. Faversham Wardmote Book. 1633-1680. KHLC. Ref. Fa/AC4 pt.1.
189. Canterbury Freemen. Op. Cit.
190. Faversham Town Books. Op. Cit.
191. Faversham Town Books. Op. Cit.
192. Faversham Muster Books. Op. Cit.
193. Faversham Port Books. 1628 & 1629. NA. Ref. E190/653/7 & 565/6.
194. Will 1624. KHLC. Ref. PRC 17/66 f.120.
195. Brewers Fines. Op. Cit. 1645.
196. Deeds. KHLC. Ref. Rigden/Whitbread. U.3555. Faversham Manor Rental. 1653. KHLC. Ref. U390. M43. Brewers Fines. Op. Cit.

197. Brewers Fines. Op, Cit. Will. KHLC. PRC 3/36 f.179.
198. Brewers Fines. Op. Cit.
199. Faversham Port Books. NA. Ref. E190/659/4.
200. Probate Inventory 1640. KHLC. Ref. PRC27/8/81.
201. Tun=8 Barrels: Pipe=4 Barrels: Hogshead=2 Barrels.
202. His buildings were demolished and rebuilt as showrooms and offices by the Gas Company c.1890.
203. Based upon Brewers Fines paid. Faversham Wardmote Books. Op. Cit. See Tables attached.
204. See: James Greenstreet. Pedigree of the Ancient Kent Family of Greenstreet and Memorials of the Ancient Kent Family of Greenstreet. Both published c.1875.
205. Brewers Fines. Op. Cit.
206. Probate Inventories & Accounts are the sole sources of data but these are inherently selective as they were not drawn up after every death. I am grateful to Linda Taylor for allowing me to copy the mid-seventeenth century Inventories she used for her article on literacy in Faversham in the seventeenth century.
207. Probate Inventory. KHLC. Ref. PRC11/4/58.
208. Probate Inventory. KHLC. Ref. PRC11/5/2.
209. Probate Inventory. KHLC. Ref. PRC11/3/41.
210. Probate Inventory. KHLC. Ref.PRC11/2/78.
211. These % are comparable as the type of households had not altered.
212. For a full discussion of population trends see Wrigley and Schofield. Population of England from 1541.
213. Faversham Port Books. Op. Cit. NA. Ref. E190/647/8.
214. Faversham Port Books. Op. Cit. NA. Ref. E190/650/1.
215. Faversham Port Books. Op. Cit. NA. Ref. E190/653/5.
216. Faversham Port Books. Op. Cit. NA. Ref. E190/655/4.
217. Arden of Faversham. Lists. Op. Cit.
218. Faversham Manor Rentals 1604 and 1653. Op. Cit.
219. Faversham Victuallers Recognisances. KHLC. Ref. Fa JQr 2.
220. Faversham Port Books. Op. Cit.
221. Faversham Port Books. NA. Ref. E190/647/8.
222. Faversham Port Books. NA. Ref. E190/650/1.
223. The lists show that bags were of various sizes. 1 Pocket = 1 3/4 cwt. 1 Small Bag=2cwt. 1 Large Bag=4cwt. The value of 1 cwt. was £7.
224. Cit. Supra.
225. Faversham Port Books. NA. Ref. E190/653/5 & 657/7.
226. Faversham Port Books. NA. Ref.E190/660/6.
227. Cit. Supra.
228. Probate Inventory. Op. Cit.
229. See E. Jacob. Map of Faversham. c.1750. Various copies displayed in The Mayor's Parlour, Faversham.
230. Faversham Manor Rental. 1653. Op, Cit. The manor rents paid probably indicate the relative sizes of the holdings: Castlocke £1.4.3, Greenstreete 4/5, Finch 12/- and Tomlin 1/5.
231. Faversham Wardmote Book. 1579-1633. Op. Cit.
232. Faversham Victuallers Recognisances. Op. Cit.
233. Faversham Presentments. KHLC. Ref. Fa/JV 55 and Fa/JQs 41.
234. Faversham Borough Records. KHLC. Ref. Fa/Jm.14.
235. B. Dietz. The Port and Trade of Early Elizabethan London. London Record Society. 1972. Based on NA. Ref. E/190/4/2.
236. Faversham Port Books. NA. Ref. E190/651/11. Ellias Maurois, ( Mr Alien) of Flushing was the main shipper.
237. Faversham Port Books. NA. Ref. E190/653/7.
238. Faversham Port Books. NA. Ref.E190/658/10.
239. Canterbury Marriage Licences.
240. Canterbury Quarter Sessions. KHLC. Ref. Q/SR/1/m.3.
241. Louis A Knafla. Kent at Law. 1602. pp.521 & 521.
242. Faversham Wardmote Book. 1579-1633. Op. Cit.
243. Faversham Wardmote Book. 1633-1651. Op. Cit.
244. Faversham Wardmote Books. Op. Cit.
245. Louis A Knafla. Kent at Law, 1602. Local Jurisdictions. Vol II. Part One. List and Index Society. Special Volume 45. 2011.
246. Kentish Gazette. 18 August 1797. University of Kent Microfilm Library.
247. Harleian Society. Grantees of Arms . British Museum Ref. Add. MSS 12225 f.23.
248. Robert Hilton. Will. KHLC. Ref. PRC17/66 f.25 : John Hilton. Will. KHLC. Ref. PRC17/67 f.29.
249. Will. KHLC. PRC17/63 f.244.
250. Will. KHLC. Ref. PRC17/59 f.417/421.
251. Will. NA. Ref. PROB11/218 f.514.
252. Will. NA. Ref. PROB11/224 f.38.
253. A. M. Everitt. The Community of Kent and the Great Rebellion. 1640-1660. pp. 188-267.
254. Faversham Wardmote Book. 1633-1651. KHLC. Ref. Fa/Ac3.

## Chapter Five

255. TNA. Chancery Exhibit. Ref. C5/384 Number 71. I am most grateful to Duncan Harrington for showing me this.
256. This Thomas became a Faversham maltster and Common Councillor, and died in 1702. His son, another Thomas, gentleman, married Christian Giles of Sheldwich and from their son, Giles Hilton of Lords at Sheldwich, the present Hilton family descends. P. Selby. The Faversham Farmers Club. 1927.
257. Faversham Manor Rentals. 1660. KHLC. Ref. U390. M.44.
258. Berry. Genealogies of Kent p.323.
259. Faversham Wardmote Book. 1654-1682.KHLC. Ref. Fa Ac 4.
260. Original Will. 1667. KHLC. Ref. PRC16/278.
261. See: Brewers Fines. Table 3.
262. Rev J Lewis. History of Faversham. 1727. p13.
263. Will. KHLC. Ref. PRC17/73 f.237.
264. See also: Burke. Dictionary of Landed Gentry. 4th. Edition. 1863.
265. I am grateful to David Steed of Spratling Court, Manston, Kent, for alerting me to this connection.
266. G. S. Johnson. History of East Langdon. pp.10-13.
267. Faversham Manor Rental. 1672. KHLC. Ref. U390.M 46.
268. Faversham Manor Rental. 1680. KHLC. Ref.U390. M 47.
269. See: Brewers Fines (Table 3).
270. Faversham Manor Rental. 1689. KHLC. Ref.U390. M 48 1/2 and Brewers Fines.
271. Faversham Manor Rental. 1711. KHLC. Ref.U390.M 49.
272. Faversham Parish Church, Churchwardens Accounts from 1699. Canterbury Cathedral Archives. Canterbury.
273. A. N. Bax. A Bax Family of East Kent. 1950.
274. Brewers Fines. Op. Cit.
275. Wills. KHLC. Refs. PRC 32/57 fs.201 & 221.

276. Copy of Marriage Settlement of Stephen Bax to Sarah Lynch 9 April 1712. Deeds of 13 Preston St. Faversham Society Collection.
277. Canterbury Marriage Licences. CCA.
278. Sun Insurance Company Policy. Guildhall Library. London. Ref. Vol. 87. No. 116757.
279. See names distribution in Kent Wills Indexes.
280. His monument is high up at the west end of the north aisle in the Faversham Parish Church.
281. Sun Insurance Company Policy Books. Guildhall Library. Refs. Vol. 54. No. 82223. Vol. 87. No. 116757.
282. Op. Cit. Policy No. 118118.
283. Deeds. 33/34 Abbey Street, Faversham. Conveyance and Release of Dower. 1769. Author's Collection.
284. See Harrington and Hyde Faversham Muster Lists and Hearth Tax Lists Op. Cit.
285. Faversham Manor Rental 1683. KHLC. Ref. U390/M. Deeds. 13 Preston Street, Faversham. 1696. Conveyance. Faversham Society Collection.Deeds. 33/34 Abbey Street, Faversham. 1769. Conveyance and Release of Dower. Author's Collection.
286. Deeds. Op. Cit.
287. Because of the details provided by The Brewers Fines and the changes of names and amounts each paid the assumption is that they reflect accurately the production of all Faversham brewers.
288. See Tables 3 & 5. Harrington & Hyde. Faversham Hearth Tax. Op. Cit. Faversham Manor Rental. 1665. KHLC. Ref. U390 M. 45.
289. Probate Inventory. Archdeacons Court Canterbury. CCA.
290. P. Mathias. Op. Cit. Table 37. p.542.
291. The samples have been taken from Probate Inventories at KHLC Ref. PRC 11. For 1660-1670, 156 survive. For 1670-1680, 127 survive. For 1690-1700, 120 survive.
292. Sun Insurance Policies. Guildhall Library London. Vol. 32. No. 53152 and No. 58281. The Sun Fire Office was the largest fire insurance company in England by 1740.
293. Probate Inventory of George Sondes. 1676. Rockingham Castle, Northamptonshire, Archive.
294. Faversham Port Books. NA Ref. E190. Samples for 1656, 1662/3, 1670/1, 1675, 1688/9, 1691/2 and 1693/4.
295. Faversham Port Books. 1662/3. Coastal trade. NA. Ref. E 190/661/8.
296. Faversham Port Books. 1681 and 1682. Overseas trade. NA. Refs. E190/666/4&9.
297. Faversham Probate Inventories. KHLC. PRC.
298. Sun Insurance Co. Guildhall Library, London. Policy No 54641. 1 July 1731. Hilles Hobday. Second husband of Mary Marsh (nee Bax).
299. Probate Inventory. James Baldock. Beer Brewer. 1673. KHLC. Ref. PRC11/35/15.
300. Probate Inventory. KHLC. Ref. PRC
301. Probate Inventory. KHLC. Ref. PRC
302. 12 Probate Inventories of Victualler Brewers survive for the years 1660-1699. KHLC. Refs. PRC
303. Cit. Supra.
304. Probate Inventory. KHLC. Ref. PRC2//26 f.102.
305. Based on a sample of 57 Probate Inventories 1660-1680 at KHLC.
306. Lees Court Inventory. 1677. Rockingham Castle, Northamptonshire. Ref. Sondes/Watson Collection.
307. Wrigley and Schofield. Op. Cit. 1650 population given as 5m; 1675 as 4.75m; 1700 as 5m; and 1725 as 5.5m.
308. This is the method of 'back projection' used by Wrigley and Schofield.
309. See Probate Inventory above.
310. See Baldock, Bax and Higgs Probate Inventories above.
311. Probate Inventory. PRC11/18 f.147. KIngsfield was the area south west of the town and north of the London Road.
312. Probate Inventory. Op. Cit.
313. P. Wilkinson. Historical Development of the Port of Faversham. p.141.
314. London MetropolitanArchives/Corporation of London Record Office. Ref. 86c. 1734/35. For the same period Sandwich sent to London 6400 quarters of malt but only 890 quarters of barley to London.
315. Probate Inventories. Cit.Supra.
316. Sun Insurance Policy. Guildhall Library. Ref. MSS. 11936. Volume 6. 20 May 1717.
317. Sun Insurance Policy. Guildhall Library. Ref. MSS. 11936. Volume 10. 23 January 1722.
318. Faversham Parish Churchwardens Assessments. 1705. CCA. Ref. P126. 11/1.
319. No Probate Inventories of Victualler Brewers, Victuallers and Innholders list malt houses.
320. Note 127 Cit. Supra.
321. Chalklin and Baker. Op. Cit.
322. Francis Gruber was the operator of The Home Gunpowder Works near Stonebridge. He was an entrepreneur rather than a craftsman powder maker.
323. Faversham Parish Church Wardens Assessments. 1725. CCA. Ref. P146.
324. Faversham Parish Church Wardens Assessments. 1732. CCA.
325. Preston Parish Tithe Books. 1731-1759. CCA. Ref. U3/249/3.
326. Preston Farm was about 80 acres in total between Faversham Station and the London Road. Deeds of Alfred House and The Crown and Anchor. Shepherd Neame Archive.
327. Plan of Faversham by Edward Jacob. 1745. Copies in Mayors Parlour, Preston Street.
328. Preston Parish Tithe Books. Op. Cit.
329. Probate Inventory. KHLC. Ref. PRC11/80 f.60.
330. Faversham Port Books. E122/232/18, E190/661/8, E190/670/4, E190/671/2 & 9, E190/677/4, E190/678/17, E190/718/23. A.M. Millard in Weights and Measures from London Port Books. NA. calculates a sack of hops weighed 2 1/2 cwt but does not define a bag.
331. Sun Fire Insurance. LMA. Policy Refs. 74279 and 75459.
332. Freemen of Canterbury. Op. Cit.
333. Faversham Borough Archives. KHLC. Ref. Fa/JQr 2 and onwards. No licenses survive for 1662-1690. Thereafter annual returns survive.
334. Faversham Manor Rentals. 1660 to 1744. Op. Cit. KHLC. Ref. U390. M44 onwards.
335. Faversham Manor Rentals. Op. Cit.
336. Deeds. Shepherd Neame Archive.
337. See. J Owen. The Shepherds of Shepherd Neame Brewery Faversham. 1732-1876.
338. Probate Account. 1682. KHLC. Ref. PRC2/40 f.134.
339. Probate Account. 1679. KHLC. Ref. PRC2/36 f.247.

340. Probate Accounts. KHLC. Refs. PRC2.
341. Probate Inventory. KHLC. Ref. PRC11/35 f.202.
342. Probate Inventory. KHLC. Ref. PRC11/60 f.176.
343. Probate Inventory. 1673. Richard Foster. KHLC. Ref. PRC11/35 f.80.
344. National Archives.
345. Evelyn Papers. British Library. Ref. Add. Ms. 79,398. ff.1-16. John Evelyn was a Commissioner for Sick and Wounded Seamen and kept very detailed accounts.
346. Probate Inventory. Op.Cit.
347. DNW Sale Catalogue. 16 March 2005. Robert Hogarth Kent Tokens Collection. Faversham Lot No. 1163.
348. Faversham Poor Assessments. 1722-1729. CCA. Ref.U3/P146/11/3.
349. Faversham Wardmote Book. Wine Licence entries for each year KHLC. Ref. Fa.
350. Faversham Manor Rentals. 1711, 1717 and 1743. KHLC. Ref. U390. M.
351. Deeds. Authors Library.
352. E. Jacob. History of Faversham. List of Mayors.
353. For accounts of these few days see: E. Jacob. History of Faversham. pp.205-213. James II Coming to Faversham by Capt. Richard Marsh. and E. Beddard. A Kingdom without a King.
354. This survived until at least 1960 in a small glass case in the Vicar's Vestry in the Parish Church. It has since disappeared.
355. Calendars of State Papers. 1689-1702. NA.
356. Burke. Dictionary of the Landed Gentry. 4th. Edition. 1863.
357. Will. KHLC. Ref. PRC17/86 f.27.
358. NA. Ref. PROB11/799 ff.169/173.
359. P. York. Diary of John Baker. Barrister at Law. 1933. p.97.
360. Thomas Tompion was the leading watch and clock maker of his day.
361. B. Robins. The John Marsh Journals of a Gentleman Composer, 1752-1828. John Marsh sold Nethersole in 1784.
362. The sculptor is unknown but the style of the bust is very similar to those of Robert Taylor, whose City of London clientele would have been part of the circle of both John Marsh and John Winchester.
363. Administration. KHLC. Ref. PRC
364. The Shepherds of Shepherd Neame. Op. Cit.
365. See Faversham Church, Poor and Manorial Assessments for 1705-1732. Op. Cit.
366. Item 39. Exhibition of Historical Documents, Cumberland House Museum, Portsmouth. 1956. Lent by Portsmouth City Librarian. This was noted by Sidney Wilson of Faversham. CCA. Ref. S. Wilson Collection. It has since been lost by Portsmouth Library the archivist informs me.
367. The Shepherds of Shepherd Neame. Op. Cit.

# Illustrations

**Fig. 1** *Elizabethan Ale Wives*
*Sixteenth Century*
*Stained Glass.*
*Oxborough Hall, Norfolk*
*(National Trust Collection.)*

**Fig. 2** *Samuel Hayward*
*Merchant and Mayor of Faversham*
*Memorial Brass 1610*
*Faversham Parish Church*

Fig. 3 *John Castlocke IV*
*Brewer and Mayor of Faversham*
*Monument 1651*
*Faversham Parish Church*

Fig. 4 *Edward Weller*
*Brewer and Mayor of Faversham*
*Monument 1762*
*Faversham Parish Church*

**Fig. 5** *Silvester Marsh*
*Daughter of Richard Marsh jun.*
*Monument 1742*
*Faversham Parish Church*

**Fig. 6** *John Marsh*
*Eldest Son of Richard Marsh sen.*
*Bust and Monument 1752*
*Attributed to Robert Taylor*
*Woodnesborough Parish Church*

*Fig. 7 18 Court Street, Faversham*
*Shepherd Neame Brewery*
*Re-fronted 18th Century and part rebuilt 18th Century*

*Fig. 8 15/17 Preston Street, Faversham*
*Stransham, Cole & Tomlin Brewery Site*
*Rebuilt c.1600*
*Photograph c.1868*
*(Dr. Charles Turner Collection)*

**Fig. 9** *67/68 Preston Street, Faversham*
*Bax, Weller & Rigden Brewery Site*
*Re-fronted c.1770.*

**Fig. 10** *88/89 West Street, Faversham*
*Hilton & Baldock Brewery Site*
*Rebuilt c.1900*
*Photograph c.1912*

**Fig. 11** *Brew House*
*Lacock Abbey, Wiltshire*
*Sixteenth Century*
*(National Trust Collection)*

**Fig. 12** *Brew House*
*Early Eighteenth Century*
*Engraving*

**Fig. 13** *Small Brew House 1748* *(Universal Magazine)*

**Fig. 14** *Tun Cask Coopers c. 1500 Engraving*

**Fig. 15** *Mediaeval Tavern Interior*
*Mediaeval Manuscript*

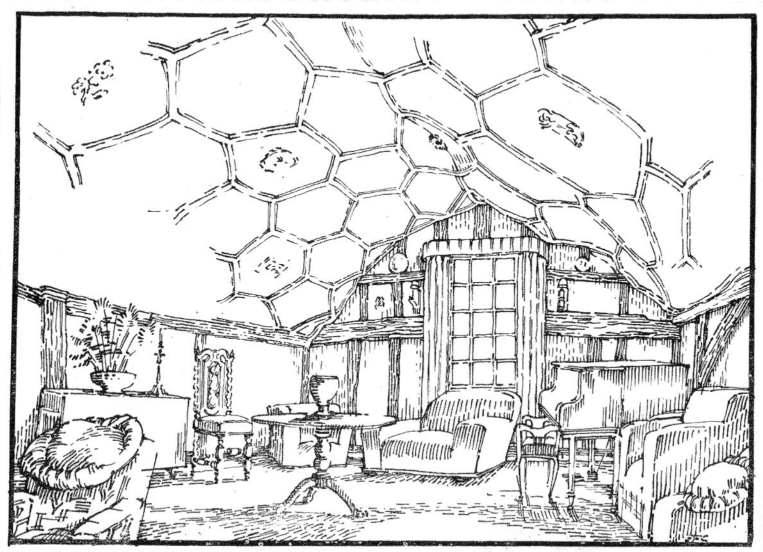

**Fig. 16** *The Ship Hotel*
*16 Market Place, Faversham*
*Elizabethan Ceiling*
*Sketch c. 1950*

**Fig. 17** *The Fleur de Lys*
*14 Market Place, Faversham*
*Mediaeval Yard Range*
*Now Hugh Place*
*(Dr. Arthur Percival Collection)*

**Fig. 18**
*The Greyhound*
*6-9 West Street,*
*Faversham*
*Refronted in parts*
*Photograph c. 1895*
*(Faversham Society Crosoer Collection)*

**Fig. 19** *The Castle*
*76 West Street, Faversham*
*Photograph c. 1930*

**Fig. 20**
*The Three Tunns*
*Tanners Street,*
*Faversham*
*Photograph c.1890*
*(Frank Crosoer Collection Faversham Society)*

**Fig. 21** *Tying the Hop Bines*
*R. Scott*
*Perfite Platform of a Hop Garden 1570*
(B. Wright Collection)

**Fig. 22** *Cutting the Hop Bines*
*R. Scott*
*Perfite Platform of a Hop Garden 1570*
(B. Wright Collection)

**Fig. 23** *Hop Poles*
*Stacks*
*1750*
*Angerstein Diary*

**Fig. 24** *Hop Yard*
*Homestall Farm, Faversham*
*c.1590*
*Saxton Map*
*(KHLC. U390. P2. Collection)*

**Fig. 25** Token *1/2d*
*Robert Hogben*
*Three Tunns, West Street*
*1655*
*(Faversham Society Collection) (Clive Foreman photo)*

**Fig. 26** *Token 1/2d*
*John Cleare*
*The Crown, West Street*
*1666*
*(Faversham Society Collection) (Clive Foreman photo)*

# Maps

**Map 1** *The Brewery Sites. 1600.*
*Faversham Town Map.*
*5 known sites. 3 identified sites.*

**Map 2** *The Brewery Sites. 1700.*
*Faversham Town Map.*
*6 known sites. 4 identified sites.*

**Map 3** *Public Houses. 1604.*
*Faversham Town Map.*
*18 known sites. 10 identified sites.*

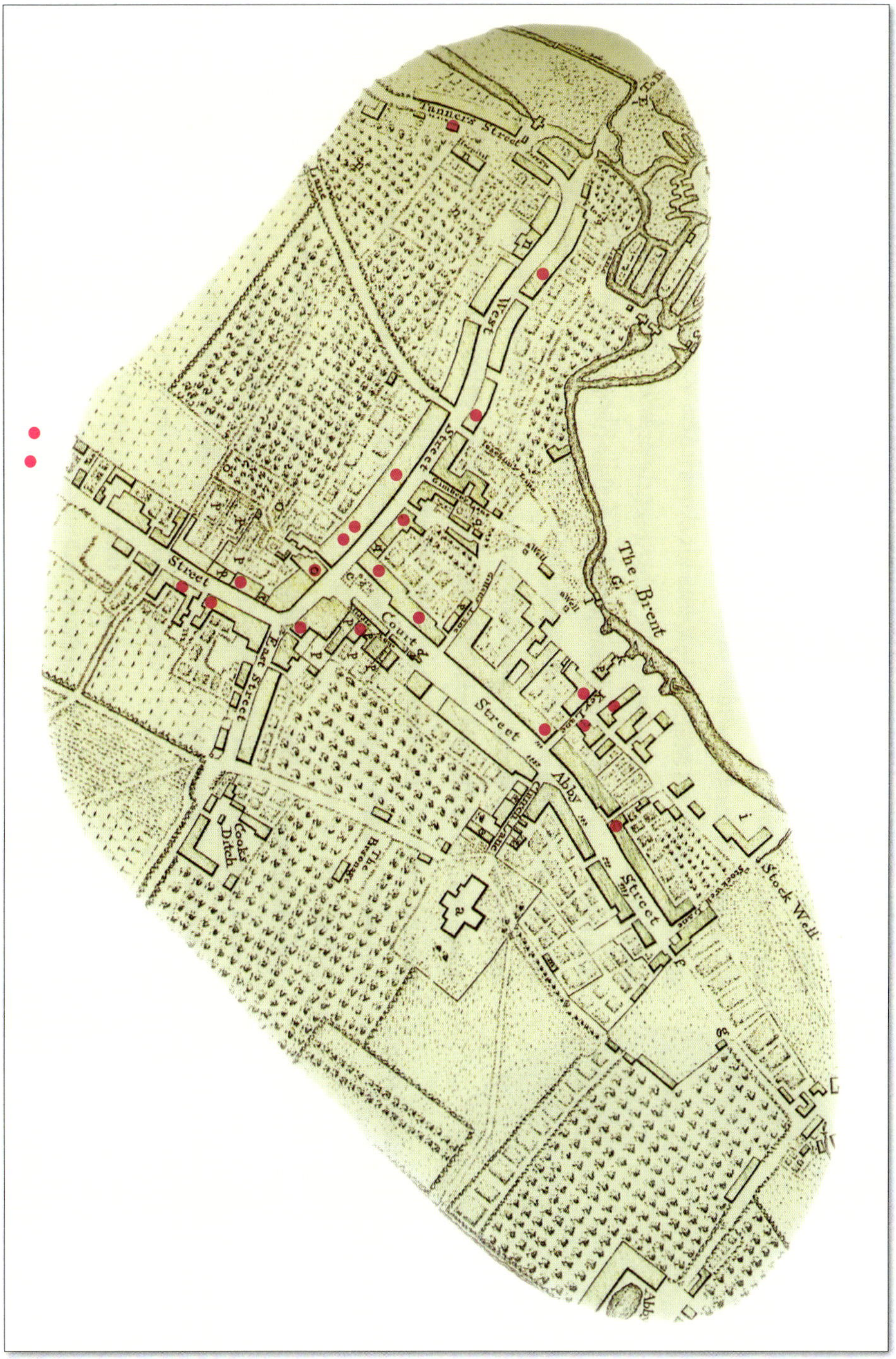


**Map 4** *Public Houses. 1710.*
*Faversham Town Map.*
*24 known sites. 22 identified sites.*

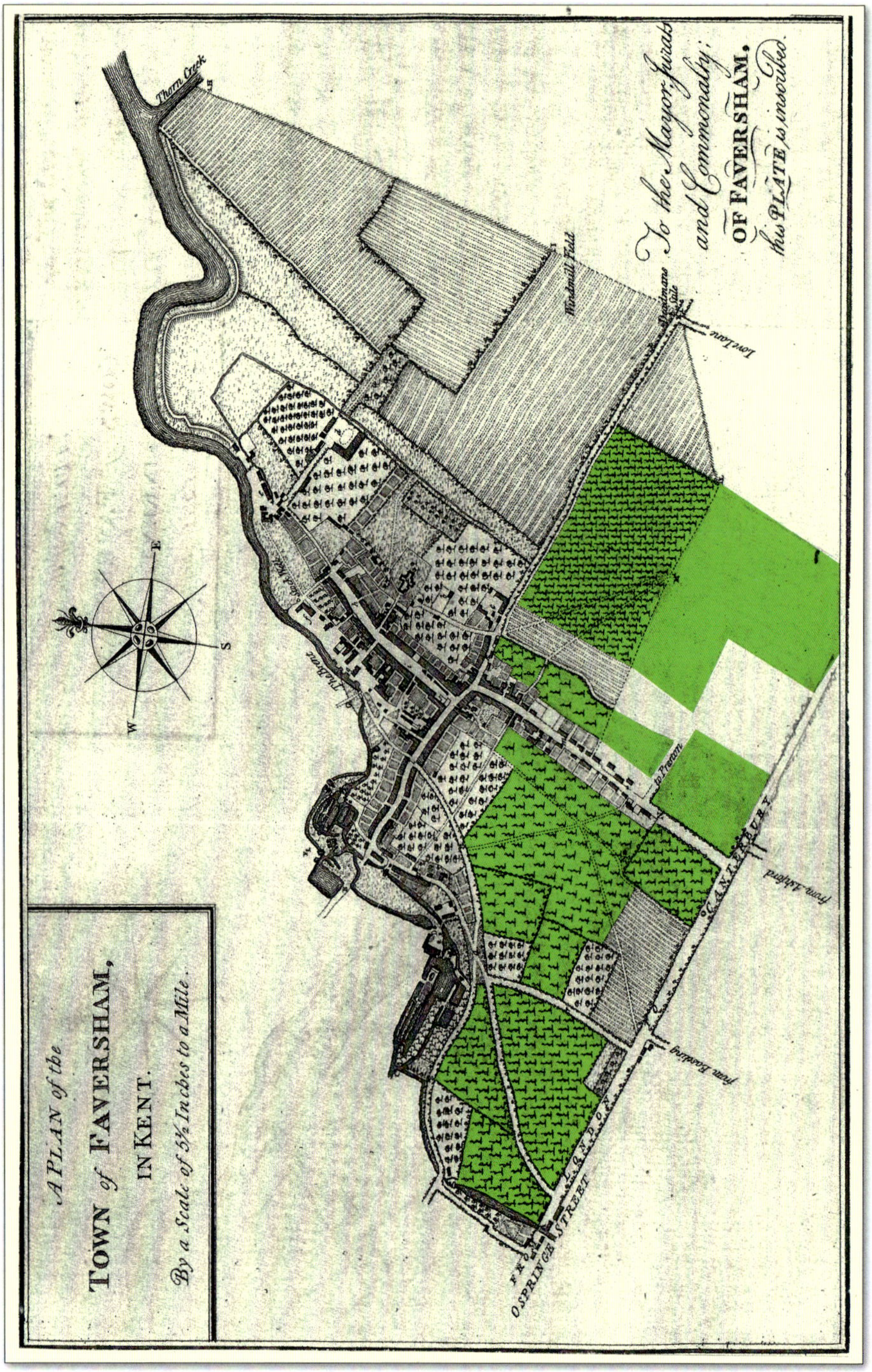


**Map 5** *Plan of Faversham by Edward Jacob 1745*
*Hop Gardens*

# Tables

**Table 1.** *Faversham Brewers, Innkeepers and Tipplers 1327*

| | Names | Tax Amounts |
|---|---|---|
| **Brewsters (Braciatrices)** | | |
| Wife of | Stephen Teghelere | 12d 6d |
| Relict of | Thomas Sclerer | 12d 6d |
| | Adde Langyndon | 12d |
| | Mauld de Hame | 12d |
| Daughter of | Laurance le Hyare | 12d |
| Wife of | Thomas de Gravene | 18d |
| | Elena Badecok | 8d |
| Wife of | William de Dovare | 6d |
| Wife of | Richard de Gravene | 4s |
| | Johana de Hanekernesse | 12d 6d |
| | Mauld Lau'anc | 6d |
| | Dyonis Merchalis | 6d |
| Wife of | John de Makynhanede | 2s 6d 6d |
| Relict | Radulph Note | 3s |
| Wife of | John de Maghefelde | 2s 6d 6d |
| Wife of | John Barbour | 12d 6d |
| Wife of | Stephen de Upmanton | 3s |
| Wife of | John Rodland | 6d |
| Wife of | John Revyn | 12d |
| Wife of | William Barbour | 12d |
| Wife of | Philip Note | 4s |
| Wife of | Thomas Dagh | 4s |
| Wife of | William Cok | 6d |
| Relict of | Peter Havyn | 6d |
| Maid of | Alice Beauflour | 2s |
| Wife of | Robert Sarre | 12d |
| Wife of | John Onobeth | 12d 6d |
| Wife of | Robert Neel | 2s 6d |
| Wife of | Richard att Wode | 3s |
| Wife of | Richard Taylour | 12d 6d |
| Wife of | John Cherleman | 12d |
| Wife of | Stephen Dreylonde | 3s |
| Wife of | Osbert Seman | 12d 6d |
| Wife of | Thomas Cherleman | 12d |
| Wife of | William Blakeman | 2s 6d |
| Wife of | William le Hwyte | 12d 6d |
| Wife of | Galfridus Cherleman | 2s 6d |
| Wife of | Simon de Truleghe | 6d |
| Wife of | William att fforstalle | 4s 6d |
| Relict of | John Bealdeloch | 18d |
| Wife of | John ffredle | 18d 6d |
| Wife of | Thomas att Wydereade | 12d |
| Wife of | Gilbert Noreys | 3s |
| Wife of | Philip Compyn | 3s |
| Wife of | William att Pette | 6d |
| Relict of | Roger de Bronston | 4s |
| Wife of | Thomas Sywen | 12d 6d |
| Wife of | Hamon Scharp | 12d 6d |
| Wife of | John att fforstalle | 3s |
| Wife of | Roger de Holmanston | 12d 6d |
| Wife of | Roger Deghere | 12d 6d |
| Wife of | Peter Seman | 3s |
| Relict of | William de Chalsloke | 6d |
| Wife of | Robert de Sillgrave | 4s 12d |
| Wife of | Gilbert le Smyth | 12d 6d |
| Wife of | Laurence Blabbere | 2s 6d |
| Wife of | John Rysshemere | 2s 6d |
| Wife of | Robert Dod | 4s |
| Wife of | Peter sshipman | 2s 6d 6d |
| Wife of | Stephen att Melle junior | 6d |
| Wife of | John Benynfielde | 4s |
| | Joan de Chalsloke | 6d |
| Daughter of | Richard le ffoghelere | 2s |
| Wife of | Richard Hereward | 3s |
| Wife of | Richard Archer | 12d |
| Relict of | John Goldwyne | 18d 6d |
| Wife of | John Bele | 18d 6d |
| Wife of | William de Colechestre | 18d 6d |
| Wife of | Richard att Wyk | 6d |
| Wife of | John Sperwe | 12d 6d |
| Wife of | Thomas Croucheman | 4s |
| | Alicia att Wode | 6d |
| Wife of | William de Brenle | 12d 6d 6d |
| Relict of | Alain atte fforde | 12s 6d |
| Wife of | Richard Dreylonde | 12d |
| Wife of | Mathew Bochier | 12d 6d |
| | Alicia Badecok | 12d |
| Wife of | Edmund att Hende | 6d |
| | Mauld Dreylonde | 6d |
| Wife of | Walter Seroak | 18d 6d |
| Wife of | Robert Newman | 8d 4d |
| Wife of | Thomas Badecok | 12d |
| Wife of | Robert Tannere | 9d 3d |
| Wife of | Robert Deghere | 4s |
| Wife of | Laurence Tannere | 18d 6d |
| Wife of | John Keltre | 12d |
| Relict | John Heyward | 8d 4d |
| (86 Names) | | |
| **Innkeepers (Tabernar)** | | |
| | Thomas de Brenle | 4s |
| Relict of | Randolph Note | 12d |
| (2 Names) | | |
| **Tipplers (Potcatertes)** | | |
| Wife of | John Fynche | 4d 2d |
| Wife of | Roger Opekuyne | 4d |

**Table 1.** *Faversham Brewers, Innkeepers and Tipplers 1327 (cont.)*

| | | |
|---|---|---|
| | Robert Brevecour | 4d |
| | Walter Poynant | 6d |
| | Geoffrey Goldwyne | 6d |
| | Robert Payn | 6d |
| | William Carpynter | 3s |
| | Richard Bealde | 3s |
| | Andrew Chapman | 12d 6d |
| | Richard Coupere de Moleshe | 4d 2d |
| | William Olefyer | 12d 6d |
| | Walter Copyn | 4d 2d |
| | Juliana de la Capele | 12d |
| | Henry Andrew | 12d 6d |
| | William Barbour senior | 4d 2d |
| | Hamon de Teryndenne | 8d 4d |
| | Robert de la Gayole | 4d |
| | Thomas de Stoke | 4d 2d |
| | John Taylour | 8d 4d |
| | John Lyenham | 4d |
| | John Sadelere | 4d |
| | Roger de Stalisfelde | 4d |
| | Godmus Taylour | 8d |
| | William Rycheman | 4d 2d |
| | Clement Taylour | 4d 2d |
| | William Fox | 8d |
| | William Dershere | 4d 2d |
| | Johanna Poynant | 4d 2d |
| | Hamon Dagh | 6d |
| | Arnold Smyth | 4d |
| | Richard Frode | 4d 2d |
| | William de Herthlope | 8d 4d |
| | John Coupere | 4d 2d |
| | Thomas Lokyere | 4d |
| | Thomas atte fforstalle | 8d |
| | Petyt John | 6d 4d |
| | Elbod de Noreys | 4d 2d |
| | Robert Horsman | 4d 2d |
| | Thomas Teghelere | 6d 4d |
| | Peter Teghelere | 4d |
| | Walter Teghelere | 8d |
| | John Newman | 4d |
| | Robert Dompek | 4d |
| | Lytil John | 4d |
| | Goode Boterestre | 4d 2d |
| | Robert Rycheman | 8d |
| | Roger Dorman | 8d 4d |
| | William Bakere | 8d 4d |
| | William Smyth | 4d |
| Relict of | Gilbert de Wynch | 4d |
| | Thomas atte Cruche | 6d 4d |
| | William Coreour | 4d 2d |
| | John Heyroun | 8d 4d |
| | John Hamme | 4d 2d |
| | Stace le Webbe | 4d |
| | Robert le Glovere | 4d |
| | John Geldeborne | 12d 6d |
| | John Pynke | 4d 2d |
| Relict of | Stephen Overey | 4d 2d |
| | Roger de Foxtone | 4d |
| | Henry de Ewelle | 18d 18d |
| | John Follere | 6d |
| | Thomas Colechestre | 12d |
| | William Raffe | 4d |
| | John Coreour | 4d |
| | Henry Olefyer | 4d |

(66 Names)

**Bakers (Pistor)**

(10 Names)

**Butchers (Carnifices)**

(26 Names)

**Fishermen (Piscari)**

(15 Names)

**Selling at Windows (Squallestri ffeneserage)**

(34 Names)

**Tanners (Tannater)**

(8 Names)

**Kingsmill**

(2 Names)

**Colemannishole**

(1 Name)

Source: *Tallage*
Ref: *KHLC Fa/RTz 2/1 & 2*

Table 2. *Faversham Brewers 1327-1620*

| Dates | Name | Address | Type | Servants | Source | | |
|---|---|---|---|---|---|---|---|
| **To 1400** | | | | | | **To 1400** | |
| 1327 | 86 Names | Unknown | Brewsters | | Tallage | Total Brewers Names | 86 |
| | See Table 1 | | | | | | |
| **1400 - 1450** | | | | | | **1400 - 1450** | |
| 1450 | William Barbour | 15/17 Preston St. | Brewer | | Arch. Cant. VII p 233 | Total Brewers Names | 4 |
| 1441, 1463, 1466 | | | Mayor | | | Major Brewers | 4 |
| 1450 | Richard Brayton | | Brewer | | Arch. Cant. VII p 233 | Minor Brewers | 0 |
| 1436, 1445, 1456 | | | Mayor | | | Servants | 0 |
| 1450 | Simon Orwell | | Brewer | | Arch. Cant. VII p 233 | Mayors | 4 |
| 1437 | | | Mayor | | | | |
| 1476 | | | | | Will PRC17/2 f.461 | | |
| 1450 | John Seyncler | | Brewer | | Arch. Cant. VII p 233 | | |
| 1438,1432, 1447,1448 | | | Mayor | | | | |
| **1450 - 1500** | | | | | | **1450 - 1500** | |
| 1450 | John Orwell/ Orpwell | | Brewer | | Arch. Cant. VII p.233 | Total Brewers Names | 4 |
| 1462, 1466 | | | Mayor | | | Major Brewers | 4 |
| 1462 | | | Sold Ale | | Cinque Port Books | Minor Brewers | 0 |
| 1463 | | 15/17 Preston St. | | | Fav. Leiger Book p.69 | Servants | 0 |
| ?? | Simon Orwell jun ? | | ? | | Will of SO senior | Mayors | 2 |
| 1474 | William Thornton | Preston St. | Brewer | | Fav. Leiger Book | | |
| 1466, 1473 | Nicholas Warnecourt ? | | ? | | Adm. PRC17/320 | | |
| 1473 | | | Mayor | | | | |
| 1496 | Simon Warmecourt | | Brewer | | Will PRC17/6 f.216 | | |
| | | 2/6 Preston St. | | | Dav'n Manor Court | | |
| **1500 to 1525** | | | | | | **1500 - 1525** | |
| 1517 | Michael Hester | | Brewer | | Fav. Town Books p.104 | Total Brewers Names | 3 |
| 1511 | Laurence Stransham | 15/17 Preston St.? | Brewer | | Star Chamber Case | Major Brewers | 2 |
| | | | Mayor | | | Minor Brewers | 1 |
| 1507 | Robert Withiott | Partridge Lane | Le Brewhouse | | Fav. Leiger Book f.197 | Servants | 0 |
| 1506, 1509 | | | Mayor | | | Mayors | 2 |
| 1511 | | | | | Will PRC11/12 f.233 | | |
| **1525-1550** | | | | | | **1525 - 1550** | |
| 1525, 1527 | William Castlocke | | Beer Exporter | | Arden p.396 | Total Brewers Names | 3 |
| 1541 | | | Brewer | | Letters Papers Henry VIII | Major Brewers | 2 |
| d.1550 | | | | | Adm PRC3/12 f.52 | Minor Brewers | 1 |
| 1546 | John Castlocke I | | | | | Servants | 0 |
| 1550 | | | Beerbrewer | | Adm PRC3/12 f.52 | Mayors | 0 |
| d. 1558 ? | | | | | | | |
| 1527 | John Chantrell | | Brewer | | Fav Town Books p.121 | | |
| | | | Late of Gloucester | | | | |
| *1547-1551* | *3 Brewers Fines - No Names* | | | | *Fav. Town Books* | | |

Table 2. *Faversham Brewers 1327-1620 (cont.)*

| Dates | Name | Address | Type | Servants | Source |
|---|---|---|---|---|---|
| **1550 to 1575** | | | | | |
| 1562-1584 | Cornelius Dowman | Abbey/Court St. | Tippler/Beerbrewer | 0 | Fav. Town/Muster Books |
| 1570-1590 | Fowler Derelove | Court St. | Brewer/Servant | S | Fav. Muster Books |
| d. by 1593 | | | | | Apprentice Books Fa/RA3 |
| 1574 | John Fynch | 2/6 Preston St. ? | Brewer ? | | Dav'n. Manor Court |
| 1573 | | | Mayor | | Fav. Town Books p.344 |
| 1570, 1571 | Henry le Brewer | Preston St. end | Brewer ? | | Fav. Town Books p.516/7 |
| 1549-1569 | William Maycott | | | | Fav. Town Books |
| C 16th | | 2/6 Preston St. | Brewer/Beerhouse | | Dav'n. Manor Court |
| 1574 | Clement Oldefield | West St. | Brewer | 1 | Fav. Town/Muster Books |
| d.1571 | John Perte | | Beerbrewer | | Fav. Registers Transcripts |
| 1574/5 | Robert Shrubsole | Abbey/Court St. | Brewer | 0 | Fav. Town Books p.369, 439 |
| d.1576 | George Stransham | 15/17 Preston St. | Brewer | 4 | Will PRC17/42 f.305 |
| 1552, 1555 | Thomas Tenacre | | | | Fav. Town Books |
| C 16th | | 2/6 Preston St. | Brewer/Beerhouse | | Dav'n. Manor Court |
| by 1573-1593 | William Wilson | Preston St | Brewer/Servant | S | Will PRC17/48 f.340 |
| | *0 Brewers Fines* | | | | *Fav. Town Books* |

**1550 - 1575**

| | |
|---|---|
| Total Brewers Names | 11 |
| Major Brewers | 5 |
| Minor Brewers | 4 |
| Servants | 2 |
| Mayors | 1 |

| Dates | Name | Address | Type | Servants | Source |
|---|---|---|---|---|---|
| **1575-1600** | | | | | |
| 1580-d. 1585 | John Brooke | Abbey St./Preston St. | Brewer/Servant | S | Will PRC17/46 f.316 |
| b.1552 | John Castlocke II | | | 0, 4 | PRC39/10 f.49 Depos'n |
| d.1613 | | 18 Court St. | | | Fav.Town/ Muster Books |
| by 1577 | | | Beerbrewer | | Recognisance Fa/JQv 4 |
| 1588 | | | Mayor | | |
| by 1570 | Thomas Cole | 15/17 Preston St. | Brewer | 4, 7 | Fav. Muster Books |
| d.1593 | | | | | Will PRC17/50 f.238 |
| 1575, 1582, 1591 | | | Mayor | | |
| 1583-d.1600? | William Hilton | 24 West St. | Brewer | 1 | Fav. Muster Books |
| 1583-d.1590 | Richard Huttchyne | Preston St. | Brewer | 1, 2 | Will PRC 17/48 f.17 |
| d.1593 | Michael Join | | Beerbrewer | | Fav Registers |
| 1574-d.1578 | Henry Myller | | Brewer/Servant | S | Will PRC17/43 f.224 |
| 1580-1594? | Thomas Northe | | Brewer/Servant | S | Fav. Muster Books |
| 1580s | Michael Perryie | West St. S | Brewer | 0 | Fav. Muster Books |
| 1591 | | Court St. | | | |
| d.1583 | Richard Stransham | Preston St. | Beerbrewer | 3 | Will PROB11/66 f.15 |
| by 1573-1620? | William Tomlyn | 15/17 Preston St. | Beerbrewer | 3 | Will PRC17/63 f.244 |
| | | | | | Deeds Exchequer E.44.263 |
| 1618 | | | Mayor | | Fav. Town/Muster Books |

**1575 - 1600**

| | |
|---|---|
| Total Brewers Names | 11 |
| Major Brewers | 6 |
| Minor Brewers | 2 |
| Servants | 3 |
| Mayors | 3 |

| Dates | Name | Address | Type | Servants | Source |
|---|---|---|---|---|---|
| **1600-1620** | | | | | |
| by 1623 | John Browning | | Beerbrewer | | Const' Court Dep'n 1623 |
| b. 1575 | John Castlocke III | 18 Court Street | Beerbrewer | 4 | |
| d. 1651 | | | | | Will PROB 11/218 f.514 |
| 1628 | | | Mayor | | Fav. Town/Muster Books |
| by 1602 | John Guppy | | Beerbrewer | | Recog' Fa/JQr.2 |
| 1595-?1625 | Robert Hilton | 24 West St. | Brewer | | Will PRC17/66 f.120 |
| 1610 | Richard Marback | | Brewer | | Recog'e |
| d. 1610 | Edward Wilson | Court/Abbey St. | Common Brewer | | Will PROB6/7 f.187 |
| | | | | | Fa JV.53 42 Eliz I |
| | *0 Brewers Fines* | | | | *Fav Town Books* |

**1600 - 1620**

| | |
|---|---|
| Total Brewers Names | 6 |
| Major Brewers | 2 |
| Minor Brewers | 4 |
| Servants | 0 |
| Mayors | 1 |

Table 3. *Faversham Brewers 1622-1699*

| **1579/1622** | | **1616/7** | | **1622** | | **1625/6** | | **1626/7** | |
|---|---|---|---|---|---|---|---|---|---|
| **Brewer** | **Paid** | **Brewer** | **Paid** | **Brewer** | **Paid** | **Brewer** | **Paid** | **Brewer** | **Paid** |
| No Lists | | Unpaid fines quitted | | John Castlocke jurat | 20s | John Castlocke jurat | 22s | Mr Castlocke Jurat | 20s |
| | | | | John Hilton | 20s | John Hilton | 24s | John Hilton | 20s |
| | | | | John Scott | 20s | John Scott | 24s | John Scott | 20s |
| | | | | John Sunman | 6s 8d | William Baker | 10s | William Baker | 20s |
| | | | | Morgan Goodwyn | 6s 8d | | | | |
| | | | | William Baker | 6s 8d | | | Yearly Fine 4 Brewers | £4 |

| **1628/1633** | | **1638** | | **1641** | | **1644** | | **1645** | |
|---|---|---|---|---|---|---|---|---|---|
| **Brewer** | **Paid** | **Brewer** | **Paid** | **Brewer** | **Paid** | **Brewer** | **Paid** | **Brewer** | **Paid** |
| No Lists | | Mr Castlocke | 20s | To be collected as set out in time of Mr Napleton mayor | | Mr John Castlocke | 20s | Mr John Castlocke | 20s |
| | | Mr Windsor | 20s | | | John Greenstreete | 20s | John Greenstreete | 20s |
| | | John Scott | 20s | | | William Scott | 15s | William Scott | |
| | | William Baker | 10s | | | Richard Hilton | 5s | William Baker | |
| | | Richard Hilton | 10s | | | William Baker | 10s | Henry Coxon | |
| | | | | | | Henry Coxon | 6s 8d | Thomas Baldocke | |
| | | | | | | Thomas Baldocke | 3s 4d | Edward Wright | |
| | | | | | | More brewers in town than usually have been. New apportionment. | | [Damaged] | |

| **1649** | | **1654** | | **1655** | | **1656** | | **1657** | |
|---|---|---|---|---|---|---|---|---|---|
| **Brewer** | **Paid** | **Brewer** | **Paid** | **Brewer** | **Paid** | **Brewer** | **Paid** | **Brewer** | **Paid** |
| William Dix | 20s | Mr Thomas Hilton | 20s | Arthur Whitlock | | No List | | No List | |
| Francis Verrier | 20s | Edward Wright | 20s | Unpaid Fine | 6s 8d | | | | |
| Edward Wright | 13s 4d | Robert Dadd | 6s 8d | | | | | | |
| Arthur Whitlocke | 6s 8d | Thomas Baldocke | 5s | | | | | | |
| Thomas Burt | 6s 8d | Richard Athersen | 5s | | | | | | |
| Thomas Baldocke | 5s | Henry Leese | 6s 8d | | | | | | |
| James Baldocke | 5s | Arthur Whitlocke | 5s | | | | | | |
| Francis Casse | 3s 4d | Thomas Burt | 6s 8d | | | | | | |
| Richard Adrian | 5s | John Clare | 5s | | | | | | |
| John Clare | 5s | | | | | | | | |

Table 3. *Faversham Brewers 1622-1699 (cont.)*

### 1658

| Brewer | Paid |
|---|---|
| Thomas Baldock | [ ] |
| Sarah Hilton Wo | 12s 4d |
| Richard Atheren ? | 5s |
| Henry Leese | 10s |
| Richard [ ] | 5s |
| Rebecca Bentson | 3s 4d |
| Thomas Upton | 3s 4d |
| Robert Davison | [ ] |
| Henry Nashe | 3s 4d |
| John Clare | 3s 4d |
| [Water damaged] | |

### 1659

| Brewer | Paid |
|---|---|
| No List | |

### 1660

| Brewer | Paid |
|---|---|
| Thomas Baldock | 30s |
| Thomas Davies | 5s |
| Robert Davison | [ ] |
| Thomas Clarke Wo | 2s 6d |
| Frances Whitlocke Wo | [ ] |
| Margaret Greenstreet Wo | 2s 6d |
| John Clare | 6s 8d |
| Rebecca Bentson Wo | 2s 6d |
| Henry Leese | 8s |
| William W [ ] | 3s 4d |
| George Askewe | 6s 8d |
| Nicholas Bennett | 3s 4d |
| Thomas Upton | 3s 4d |

### 1662

| Brewer | Paid |
|---|---|
| No List | |
| **Wine Licence** | |
| Elizabeth Davies | £5 |
| To put out poor children | |

### 1662 October

| Brewer | Paid |
|---|---|
| No List | |
| **Wine Licences** | |
| Thomas Baker dec'd | |
| Mrs Davies | |
| Selling wine by retail by virtue of Statute must appear before Commissioners in London Capt Trowtes to appear on their behalf | |

### 1663

| Brewer | Paid |
|---|---|
| Thomas Baldock | 30s |
| Robert Preston | 5s |
| Robert Davison | 5s |
| Elizabeth Clarke | 2s 6d |
| Frances Whitlocke | 5s |
| Margaret Greenstreete | 2s |
| John Clare | 6s 8d |
| Rebecca Bentson | 2s 6d |
| Henry Leese | 8s |
| Nicholas Bennett | 3s 4d |
| Thomas Upton | 3s 4d |
| Robert Hogben | 6s 8d |
| [Water Damaged] | |

### 1664

| Brewer | Paid |
|---|---|
| Thomas Baldock | 40s |
| Robert Preston | 5s |
| Katherine Davison | 5s |
| Elizabeth Clarke | 2s 6d |
| Frances Whitlocke | 5s |
| John Clare | 6s 8d |
| Henry Leese | 4s |
| Nicholas Bennett | 3s 4d |
| Robert Hogben | 6s 8d |
| James Dunkin | 5s |

### 1665

| Brewer | Paid |
|---|---|
| **Wine Licences** | |
| Mr Robert Preston | |
| Anne Baker Wo | |

### 1666

| Brewer | Paid |
|---|---|
| Thomas Baldock | 42s 6d |
| Robert Preston | 5s |
| Katherine Davison Wo | 5s |
| Edward Maynard | 5s |
| John Clare | 6s 8d |
| Peckenham | 4s |
| Nicholas Bennett | 3s 4d |
| Robert Hogben | 6s 8d |
| Thomas Upton | 5s |
| **Wine Licences** | |
| Mr Robert Preston | |
| Anne Baker Wo | |

### 1666

| Brewer | Paid |
|---|---|
| Thomas Baldock | £2 6s 6d |
| Robert Preston | 5s |
| Thomas Borsely | 3s 4d |
| Edward Maynard | 3s 4d |
| John Clare | 6s 8d |
| Nicholas Bennett | 4s |
| Wo Hogben | 6s 8d |
| Anne Baker Wo | 12d |
| William Thompson | 12d |
| Thomas Upton | [ ] |

**Table 3.** *Faversham Brewers 1622-1699 (cont.)*

### 1668

| Brewer | Paid |
|---|---|
| Elizabeth Baldocke Wo | £2 6s 6d |
| Thomas Borsely | 3s |
| John Hicks | 2s 6d |
| John Clare | 3s 4d |
| Nicholas Bennett | 4s |
| Philip Davison | 4s |
| Anne Baker | 18d |
| William Thompson | 12d |
| Thomas Upton | 3s 4d |
| William Varham | 4s |
| Vincent Hills | 12d |
| John Packman | 12d |
| George Munger | 12d |
| Richard Baker | 12d |
| William Perron | 12d |
| Anne Cooke Wo | 12d |
| Gyles Turley | 12d |
| Widd Kingsmill | 12d |

### 1669

| Brewer | Paid |
|---|---|
| James Baldocke | 42s 6d |
| Thomas Borsely | 3s |
| John Hicks | 2s 6d |
| Robert Platt | 3s 4d |
| Nicholas Bennett | 4s |
| Philip Scriven | 4s |
| Anne Baker | 18d |
| William Thompson | 12d |
| Anne Hills Wo | 12d |
| Thomas Upton | 3s 4d |
| William Varham | 4s |
| John Packman | 12d |
| George Munger | 2s |
| Richard Baker | 12d |
| William Perren | 12d |
| Anne Cooke | 12d |
| Wo Turley | 6d |
| Wo Kingsmill | 12d |

### 1670

| Brewer | Paid |
|---|---|
| List as 1669 | |

### 1671

| Brewer | Paid |
|---|---|
| James Baldocke | 34s |
| John Hicks | 18d |
| Robert Platt | 4s 6d |
| Nicholas Bennett | 4s |
| Philip Scriven | 4s 6d |
| Anne Baker Wo | 2s 6d |
| William Thompson | 2s |
| Simon Downs | 2s |
| Richard Forster | 4s 6d |
| William Varham | 3s |
| George Munger | 3s |
| Nathaniel Ludsome | 2s |
| Anne Cooke Wo | 18d |
| Thomas Payne | 12d |
| Henry Jarvis | 12d |
| Henry Geery | 4s |
| Rebecca Benson Wo | 2s |
| John Bradley | 12d |
| John Fryar | 2s |

### 1672

| Brewer | Paid |
|---|---|
| James Baldocke | 40s |
| John Hicks | 6d |
| Robert Platt | 4s 6d |
| Nicholas bennett | 3s |
| Philip Scriven | 4s 6d |
| Anne Baker | 2s 6d |
| William Tomson | 3s |
| Richard Forster | 2s 6d |
| William Derham | 2s 6d |
| George Munger | 4s 6d |
| Nathaniel Ludsome | 2s 6d |
| Anne Cooke | 12d |
| Thomas Paine | 12d |
| Henry Jarvis | 12d |
| Henry Geery | 5s |
| Rebecca Benson | 2s 6d |
| Edward Tanner | 2s 6d |
| Wo Fryar | 6d |
| John Johncock | 2s 6d |

**Wine Licences**

Robert Platt

Richard Forster

### 1673

| Brewer | Paid |
|---|---|

**Wine Licences**

Robert Platt

James Baldock

### 1674

| Brewer | Paid |
|---|---|
| Amy Baldocke Wo | 33s 4d |
| Robert Platt | 4s 6d |
| Nicholas Bennett | 4s 6d |
| Philip Scriven | 4s 6d |
| Anne Baker Wo | 2s 6d |
| William Tomson | 3s |
| William Varham | 3s |
| George Munger | 3s |
| Nathaniel Ludsome | 2s |
| Anne Cooke Wo | 12d |
| Thomas Paine | 12d |
| Henry Geery | 12d |
| Rebecca Benson | 3s |
| Edward Tanner | 3s |
| Andrew Bell | 3s |
| William Virgoe | 12d |

**Wine Licences**

Robert Platt

Amy Baldocke Wo

### 1676

| Brewer | Paid |
|---|---|
| Amy Baldocke Wo | 33s 4d |
| Robert Platt | 4s 6d |
| Nicholas Bennett | 4s 6d |
| Philip Scriven | 4s 6d |
| Katherine Borsley Wo | 12d |
| Anne Thomson Wo | 3s |
| William Varham | 3s |
| George Munger | 3s |
| Nathaniel Ludsome | 2s |
| Anne Cooke Wo | 12d |
| Thomas Paine | 12d |
| Henry Geery | 8d |
| Wo Philpott | 4s |
| Edward Tanner | 3s |
| Andrew Bell | 2s 6d |
| John Denham | 12d |

### 1677

| Brewer | Paid |
|---|---|
| Edward Chapman | 33s 4d |
| Robert Platt | 4s 6d |
| Nicholas Bennett | 3s 6d |
| Philip Scriven | 4s 6d |
| Wo Borsley | 18d |
| Wo Thomson | 2s |
| William Varham | 3s |
| George Munger | 2s |
| Nathaniel Ludsome | 2s |
| Anne Cooke | 2s |
| James Cooke | 12d |
| Edward Tanner | 4s |
| Andrew Bell | 3s 6d |
| John Denham | 2s |
| Arthur Major | 2s 6d |
| Richard Sherwood | 2s |
| John Willmott | 2s 6d |
| Richard Neale | 2s |
| John Cox | 12d |
| Samuel Tooley | 12d |
| Vincent Brice | 6d |
| Nicholas Mockett | 12d |

### 1678

| Brewer | Paid |
|---|---|
| Richard Marsh | 33s 4d |
| Robert Platt | 4s 6d |
| Nicholas Bennett | 3s 6d |
| Philip Scriven | 4s 6d |
| Wo Borsley | 18d |
| Wo Thomson | 1s 6d |
| William Varham | 3s 6d |
| George Munger | 2s |
| Nathaniel Ludsome | 2s |
| Anne Cooke Wo | 6d |
| James Cooke | 12d |
| Edward Tanner | 4s 6d |
| Andrew Bell | 3s 6d |
| John Denham | 2s |
| Arthur Major | 2s 6d |
| Richard Sherwood | 2s |
| John Willmott | 2s 6d |
| Richard Neale | 2s |
| John Cox | 12d |
| Samuel Tooley | 12d |
| Vincent Brice | 6d |
| Nicholas Mockett | 12d |
| John Philpott | 6d |
| Richard Ashby | 6d |

Table 3. *Faversham Brewers 1622-1699 (cont.)*

| **1679** | | **1680** | | **1681** | | **1682** | | **1683** | |
|---|---|---|---|---|---|---|---|---|---|
| **Brewer** | **Paid** | **Brewer** | **Paid** | **Brewer** | **Paid** | **Brewer** | **Paid** | **Brewer** | **Paid** |
| | | Richard Marsh | 36s 8d | Richard Marsh | 36s 4d | Richard Marsh | 36s 8d | Not copied | |
| **Wine Licences** | | | | | | Robert Platt | 5s | | |
| Robert Platt | | Not copied | | Not copied | | Philip Scriven | 5s | **Wine Licences** | |
| Philip Scriven | | | | | | Katherine Borsley | 12d | Robert Platt | £5 |
| | | | | | | William Varham | 3s | Philip Scriven | £5 |
| | | | | | | Edward Gossum | 1s 6d | | |
| | | | | | | Nathaniel Ludsome | 1s 6d | | |
| | | | | | | Edward Tanner | 2s | | |
| | | | | | | Richard Neale | 3s | | |
| | | | | | | Katherine Major Wo | 3s | | |
| | | | | | | Richard Sherwood | 2s | | |
| | | | | | | William Whiteridge | 5s | | |
| | | | | | | Samuel Tooley | 12d | | |
| | | | | | | Mary Brice Wo | 2s 6d | | |
| | | | | | | Nicholas Mockett | 12d | | |
| | | | | | | John Philpott | 2s | | |
| | | | | | | Richard Ashbey | 2s | | |

| **1684/85** | | **1685/86** | | **1686/87** | | **1687/88** | | **1688/89** | |
|---|---|---|---|---|---|---|---|---|---|
| **Brewer** | **Paid** | **Brewer** | **Paid** | **Brewer** | **Paid** | **Brewer** | **Paid** | **Brewer** | **Paid** |
| Not copied | | Not copied | | Richard Marsh | 43s | Not copied | | Not copied | |
| Inc | | Inc | | Alexander Bax | 20s | | | | |
| John Buck | 6s | Alex Bax brewer | 21s | William Varham | 2s 6d | **Wine Licences** | | **Wine Licences** | |
| | | Rich Marsh brewer | 40s | Wo Tanner | 3s | Robert Platt | £5 | William Whiting | £5 |
| | | | | William Hawker | 2s 6d | John Clarke | £5 | Thomas Higgs | £5 |
| | | | | John Major | 3s 6d | | | | |
| | | | | Mary Brice Wo | 2s 6d | | | | |
| | | | | Nicholas Mockett | 2s 6d | | | | |
| | | | | John Philpott | 2s | | | | |
| | | | | **Wine Licences** | | | | | |
| | | | | Robert Platt | £5 | | | | |
| | | | | Lease on Queens Arms 7 Years | | | | | |
| | | | | Philip Scriven | £5 | | | | |

Table 3. *Faversham Brewers 1622-1699 (cont.)*

| 1689/90 | | 1690/91 | | 1691/92 | | 1693/94 | | 1695/96 | |
|---|---|---|---|---|---|---|---|---|---|
| **Brewer** | **Paid** | **Brewer** | **Paid** | **Brewer** | **Paid** | **Brewer** | **Paid** | **Brewer** | **Paid** |
| Not copied | | Richard Marsh | £2 6s 0d | Richard Marsh | £2 6s 6d | Richard Marsh | £2 10s 0d | Richard Marsh | £2 5s 0d |
| | | Alexander Bax | £1 1s 6d | Alexander Bax | £1 1s 6d | Alexander Bax | £1 2s 6d | Alexander Bax | £1 2s 6d |
| **Wine Licences** | | Elizabeth Varham Wo | 2s | Margaret Berry Wo | 2s | Thomas Hodges | 18d | John Thomas | 2s |
| Thomas Higgs | £5 | Joane Tanner Wo | 2s 6d | Joane Tanner Wo | 1s 6d | John Thomas | 12d | Arthur Major | 2s 6d |
| Queens Arms empty | | John Thomas | 1s | John Thomas | 12d | Arthur Major | 4s | Thomas Hodges | 3s |
| | | John Major | 4s | John Major | 4s | Nicholas Mockett | 2s 6d | Mathew Denham | 2s 6d |
| | | Nicholas Mockett | 2s 6d | Nicholas Mockett | 2s | | | John Jeffery | 2s 6d |
| | | John Philpott | 2s | John Philpott | 2s 6d | | | | |
| | | Thomas Foreman | 2s 2d | | | | | | |
| | | | | **Wine Licences** | | | | | |
| | | **Wine Licences** | | Thomas Higgs | £5 | | | | |
| | | Not copied | | | | | | | |

| 1697/98 | | 1698/99 | |
|---|---|---|---|
| **Brewer** | **Paid** | **Brewer** | **Paid** |
| Richard Marsh | £2 8s 6d | Richard Marsh | £2 8s 6d |
| Alexander Bax | £1 1s | Alexander Bax | £1 4s 0d |
| John Thomas | 2s | John Hall | 2s |
| John Major | 2s 6d | John Major | 2s 6d |
| Thomas Hodges | 3s | Thomas Hodges | 3s |
| Mathew Denham | 2s 6d | Richard Glover | 3s |
| Richard Glover | 2s 6d | | |
| | | Brewers Fines | |
| Dan Glover rent for Queens Arms | | cease 1699 | |

Source: *Brewers Fines*
*Faversham Wardmote Books 1579-1699*
Refs: *KHLC Fa AC 3 & 4*

Table 4. *Faversham Brewers 1700-1730*

| Names | Dates 1700-1710 | 1711-1720 | 1721-1732 | Address |
|---|---|---|---|---|
| Alexander Bax | 1685-1702 | | | 67/69 Preston St |
| Stephen Bax | ?1709 | to ? 1715 | | 67/69 Preston St |
| Edward Weller | ?1702 | to 1750s | | 67/69 Preston St |
| Edward Rigden | | | ? 1730s | 67/69 Preston St |
| William Rigden | | | by 1739 | 67/69 Preston St |
| Thomas Higgs | 1700-1707 | | | The Ship, Market Pl |
| Richard Marsh sen. | 1678 | to 1720s | | 18 Court St |
| Richard Marsh jun. | by 1705 | to 1727 | | 18 Court St |
| Mary Marsh | | | 1727-1732 | 18 Court St |
| Hilles Hobday | | | ? 1728-1731 | 18 Court St |

Sources: *Faversham Property Deeds and Sun Fire Office Insurance Policies*
Refs: *As quoted in the text*

Table 5. *Faversham Identified Tippling Houses, Alehouses and Inns 1488-1653*

| Manorial Rent | Name | Location | Dates From | Dates To |
|---|---|---|---|---|
| | Bear | 3 Market Place | By 1488 | OPEN |
| 1/8 | Bell | 37/38 Preston Street | By 1604 | 1680s |
| 1/6 | Black Anchor | 25 Court Street | By 1503 | ?1770s |
| | Cock | Court Street ? | By 1578 | By 1604 |
| 11/8 + 2Hens | Crown | 114 West Street | By 1503 | c.1710 |
| 1/- | Dolphin | 86 Preston Street | By 1670 | 1970s |
| 2d | Falcon | 1 West Street | By 1653 | 1970s |
| 1/6 4Bs B | Fleur de Lys | 15 Market Place | By 1532 | 1680s |
| 8d | Flying Hog | 2 Court Street | c. 1660 | 1720s |
| 6d | Flying Horse | 24 West Street | By 1604 | By 1691 |
| | Greyhound | 6/9 West Street | By 1532 | By 1604 |
| 4/5 + Hen | Horne | 7/7A Market Place | By 1532 | 1680s |
| | Lion | ? | By 1561 | By 1604 |
| | Maypole | Preston Street | C16th | By 1604 |
| 1/- | Mermaid | 14 Abbey Street | c. 1660 | c. 1990 |
| 2/4 | Queens Arms | 12 Market Place | By 1593 | By 1691 |
| | Red Horse | East Street South | By 1604 | By 1653 |
| | Red Lion | Preston Street | By 1560 | By 1604 |
| | Rose | 80 Preston Street | By 1653 | By 1653 |
| 2/1 + Hen | Rose & George | 80 Preston Street | By 1532 | By 1653 |
| | Saracens Head | Preston Street East | By 1524 | By 1604 |
| | Sheers | Preston Street | By 1579 | By 1604 |
| 4/- | Ship | 16 Market Place | By 1532 | 1980 |
| | Squire | Preston Street | By 1579 | By 1604 |
| 4/- + 2 Hens | Swan | Swan Quay | 1670s | ? |
| | Swan | Preston Street West | By 1573 | By 1604 |
| 4/4 | White Horse | Court Street East | By 1608 | By 1621 |

Sources: *Faversham Manor Rentals*
*Faversham Wills*
Refs: *KHLC*

Table 6. *Faversham Tipplers, Alehouse Keepers, Inn Holders and Victuallers Recognisances 1570-1620*

| Year | Premises | Licencee | Status | Recognisanse | Status | Recog'e | Status |
|---|---|---|---|---|---|---|---|
| **1570** | | | | | | | |
| | | 17 entries | | No brewers | | | |
| | | For details see Town | | | | | |
| | | Books by Hyde | | No Castelocke | | | |
| | | & Harrington | | No Hilton | | | |
| | | | | No Stransham | | | |
| **1577** | | | | | | | |
| January | | John Skyrr | Innholder | ? | | Thomas Carlyng | Innholder |
| | | William Chapman | Tippling house keeper | ? | | ? | |
| | | Albert Johnson | Tippling house keeper | ? | | ? | |
| | | John Longley | Tippling house keeper | ? | | ? | |
| | | Peter Hollar | Tippling house keeper | ? | | ? | |
| | | William Bynge | Tippling house keeper | John Castelocke | | ? | |
| | | Robert Rye | Tippling house keeper | Robert Lane | | John Tyndale | Grocer |

Table 6. *Faversham Tipplers, Alehouse Keepers, Inn Holders and Victuallers Recognisances 1570-1620*

| Year | Premises | Licencee | Status | Recog'e | Status | Recog'e | Status |
|---|---|---|---|---|---|---|---|
| | | Abraham Snoade | Tippling house keeper | John Castelocke | | Thomas Furmynger | |
| | | Thomas Cobham | Tippling house keeper | William Todd | | Thomas Wood | |
| | | John Gausnoth | Tippling house keeper | William Todd | | Clemens Walton | |
| | | Roger Byssyngton | Tippling house keeper | William Todd | | ? | |
| | | Bokeland Braye | Tippling house keeper | ? | | ? | |
| | | Richard Cyneen | Taylor | Hugo Coothe | Grocer | Arthur Byerton | |
| | | Margery Dennys | Tippling house keeper | William Todd | | Hugo Coothe | |
| | | Thomas Hawkes | Innholder | Edward Harrys | Woollendraper | ? Boothe | Grocer |
| October | | List includes | | | | | |
| | | Abraham Snoode | Tipplinghouse keeper | John Castelocke | Beere bruer | | |
| | | William Symon | Tipplinghouse keeper | Richard Stransham | Beere bruer | | |
| | | John Amys | Innkeeper | | | | |
| | | 15 in total | | | | | |
| **1580** | | | | | | | |
| | | Abraham Snode | Tipplinghouse keeper | John Castlocke | Brewer | John Upton | Gentleman |
| October | | William Taylor | Tipplinghouse keeper | Thomas Bye | Yeoman | Stephen Anderson | Yeoman |
| | | John Hansnoode | Tipplinghouse keeper | Stephen Meere | ? | Clement ? | |
| | | John Stretton | Tipplinghouse keeper | William Cadman | ? | Robert Stretton | ? |
| | | ? | | Richard Streynsham | Brewer | Clement Walton | Blacksmith |
| | | 5 in total | | | | | |
| **1589** | | | | | | | |
| | | List includes | | | | | |
| | | John Baldocke | Tipplinghouse keeper | Richard Huttchyne | Bruer | | |
| | | William Hunt | Alehouse keeper | Michael Perryie | Bruer | | |
| | | 22 in all | | | | | |
| **1590** | | | | | | | |
| | | Nicholas Finch | Innkeeper | George Cruttall | Baker | Vincent Clarkson | ? |
| | | Thomas Saunders | Innkeeper | George Crosse | Tailor | George Cruttall | Baker |
| | | Nicholas Adye | Innkeeper | George Cruttall | Baker | Vincent Clarkson | ? |
| | | Gyles Ledgegoode | Ty ppler | Vincent Clarkson | Baker | Francis Malan | Shipwright |
| | | William Hamlyn | Victualler | George Cruttall | Baker | Vincent Clarkson | Baker |
| | | Richard ?Younte | Victualler | George Cruttall | Baker | Clement Walton | Smythe |
| | | John Baldocke | Typpler | William Tomlyn | Brewer | Vincent Clarkson | Baker |
| | | Edmund ? Lellerdon | Typpler | John Lellerdon | | ? Malam | |
| | | John Taylor | Typpler | William Hilton | Brewer | Vincent Clarkson | Baker |
| | | John Blunckett | | Vincent Clarkson | Baker | Stephen Fynne | Baker |
| | | Henry Clerke | Typpler | William Tomlin | Brewer | Vincent Clarkson | Baker |
| | | Thomas Brett | | Vincent Clarkson | Baker | George Cruttall | Baker |
| | | Robert Rye | | Vincent Clarkson | Baker | George Cruttall | Baker |
| | | Thomas Day | Typpler | Clemt Walton | Smith | George Cruttall | Baker |
| | | Andrew Danyell | | Vincent Clarkson | Baker | George Cruttall | Baker |
| | | Alice Armerer | AH & TH keeper | William Tomlyn | Brewer | George Cruttall | Baker |
| | | Andrew Daniell | AH & TH keeper | William Tomlyn | Brewer | George Cruttall | Baker |

Table 6. *Faversham Tipplers, Alehouse Keepers, Inn Holders and Victuallers Recognisances 1570-1620 (cont.)*

| Year | Premises | Licencee | Status | Recog'e | Status | Recog'e | Status |
|---|---|---|---|---|---|---|---|
| **1591** | | | | | | | |
| | | List includes | | | | | |
| | | Thomas Saunders | Innkeeper | William Tomlyn | Brewer | | |
| | | Jarman Weyghte | AH & TH keeper | William Tomlyn | Brewer | | |
| | | Alice Byrcon | AH & TH keeper | William Hylton | Brewer | | |
| | | Thomas Younge | AH & TH keeper | William Hylton | Brewer | | |
| | | Richard Monnte | AH & TH keeper | William Tomlyn | Brewer | George Cruttall | Baker |
| | | John Baldocke | Labourer | William Tomlyn | Brewer | Stephen Fynne | |
| | | John Taylor | Yeoman | William Hylton | Brewer | Clemens Trowt | Mariner |
| | | Thomas Cockes | Labourer | William Tomlyn | Brewer | George Cruttall | Baker |
| | | John Vgden | Taylor | Vincent Clarson | Baker | William Hylton | Brewer |
| | | Gyles Ledgood | Yeoman | Vincent Clarson | Baker | William Hylton | Brewer |
| | | Richard Byndon | Taylor | Vincent Clarson | Baker | William Hylton | Brewer |
| | | Henry Clere | Painter | William Tomlyn | Brwer | Richard Peasse | Butcher |
| | | 24 in all | | | | | |
| | | 3 innkeepers | | | | | |
| **1592** | | | | | | | |
| | | List includes | | | | | |
| | | Thomas Young | Vyttler | John Hampton | Taylor | William Hylton | Brewer |
| | | 23 in all | | | | | |
| **1593** | | | | | | | |
| | | 22 in all | | 4 Tomlyn recogs | | 3 Hylton recogs | |
| **1601** | | | | | | | |
| | | Gyles Ledgegood | Innkeeper | George Cruttall | Baker | Anthony Longe | |
| | | Anna Bennett | Widow | George Cruttall | Baker | William Tomlyn | Beerbrewer |
| | | Thomas Saunders | Innkeeper | George Cruttall | Baker | James Womseter ? | Maltster |
| | | John Taylor | Labourer | William Tomlyn | Beerbrewer | William Johnson | Tailor |
| | | David Parker | Miller | William Thurston | Haberdasher | Gabriel Oliver | ? Sciffer |
| | | Jerman Waight | Labourer | George Cruttall | Baker | John Halden | Basketmaker |
| | | Radus Dugglas | Taylor | William Tomlyn | Beerbrewer | George Cruttall | Baker |
| | | John Pease | Butcher | James Wanrcester | Maltster | William Johnson | Tailor |
| | | John Hutchens | Minstrel | Michael Jarman | Tailor | Robert Hylton | Beerbrewer |
| | | Barbara Welch | Widow | William Tomlyn | Beerbrewer | Jacob Warncester | Maltster |
| | | Thomas Brattle | Butcher | George Cruttall | Baker | James Womseter ? | Maltster |
| | | William Bule | Labourer | George Cruttall | Baker | Robert Hylton | Beerbrewer |
| | | William Gymson | Coller | Robert Hylton | Beerbrewer | William Cossen | Tailor |
| | | John ? Snnxe | Beerbrewer | William Tomlyn | Beerbrewer | Thomas Hamon | Sadler |
| | | Richard Hall | Shoemaker | John Caslocke jun | Gentleman | Anthony Longe | Butcher |
| | | William Dennis | Sailor | John Caslocke jun | Gentleman | John Hampton | Tailor |
| | | Thomas Sharpe | Labourer | William Thurston | Haberdasher | George Cruttall | Baker |
| | | Giles Gorham | Cooper | John Doman | Shoemaker | William Johnson | Tailor |
| | | Henry Ruggler ? | Barber | John Nevell | Barber | John Moyle | Tailor |

**Table 6.** *Faversham Tipplers, Alehouse Keepers, Inn Holders and Victuallers Recognisances 1570-1620 (cont.)*

| Year | Premises | Licencee | Status | Recog'e | Status | Recog'e | Status |
|---|---|---|---|---|---|---|---|
| 1610 | | | | | | | |
| | | David Parker | Miller | John Goldthwaight | Baker | John Pease | Butcher |
| | | Richard Lyle | Shoemaker | Richard Marback | Brewer | Abraham Browne | Shoemaker |
| | | Barbara Welch | Widow | Richard Marback | Brewer | David ? | Tailor |
| | | Gabriel Bexlie | Taylor | William Hilton | Brewer | Richard Cage | Gent |
| | | John ? | Victualler | James Lambert | Baker | William Gill | Sailor |
| | | John Willams | Wheeler | Josias Sparke | Maultman | William Jackson | Butcher |
| | | | | John Wood | | John Robins | |
| | | William Anstel | Victualler | Arnold Terry | Yeoman | Tobias Stretman | Surgeon |
| | | Walter Rand | Victualler | Stephen Harwoodd | Sailor | Richard Swanton | Sailor |
| | | John Morris | Victualler | Michael Barrons | Sailor | John Baser | Sailor |
| | | Chatborne Arrow | Glover | John Goldthwaight | Baker | William Arrowe | ? |
| | | John Douglas | Victualler | James Lambert | Baker | Thomas Clarke | tailor |
| | | Susannah Henley | Widow | William Williams | Maltman | John Crofte | Shoemaker |
| | | Phillippa Gill | Widow | Nicholas Butcher | Tailor | Richard Hamon | Carpenter |
| | | Margaret Brett | Widow | John Nevill | Barber | Henry Holman | Chandler |
| | | Alice Tailor | Widow | John Glewe | Bricklayer | Thomas Pennyale | Blacksmith |
| | | Johanna Adye | Widow | John Swaton | Grocer | Thomas Hamon | Sadler |
| | | Johanna Ledgegood | Widow | John Swaton | Grocer | John \|Cruttall | Barber |
| | | Edward Heron | Innholder | James Lambet | Baker | Thomas Platt | Joiner |
| 1620 | | | | | | | |
| | | Walter Moyses | A H & V H Keeper | Jacob Lambert | Baker | John Watson | Sailor |
| Bundle | | David Parker | A H & V H Keeper | John Everest | Innholder | Chatborne Arrow | Glover |
| | | John Watson | A H & V H Keeper | Walter Moses | Innkeeper | Jacob Lambert | Baker |
| | | William Williams | A H & V H Keeper | Jacob Lambert | Baker | William Cessin | Taylor |
| | | Marie Bootes | A H & V H Keeper | Jacob Lambert | Baker | William Cessin | Taylor |

Source: *Recognisanses (Licences)*
Ref: *KHLC Fa JQr 2*

Table 7. *Faversham Tipplers, Alehouse Keepers, Inn Holders and Victuallers Recognisances 1662*

| Christian Name | Surname | Location | Brewers Fine |
|---|---|---|---|
| Mary | Arger | ? | |
| Anne | Baker | ? | |
| Thomas | Baker | ? | |
| William | Bayly | Quays | |
| Nicholas | Bennett | Abbey St West | Brewer |
| Rebecca | Benson | Court St West | Brewer |
| Henry | Bratton | West St/Tanners St | |
| Richard | Browning | West St/Tanners St | |
| John | Clare | West St/Abbey St West | Brewer |
| Elizabeth | Clarke | Preston St West | Brewer |
| James | Cooke | West St/Tanners St | |
| Edward | Crower | Quays | |
| Elizabeth | Davies | Preston St West | |
| Robert | Davison | Preston St West | Brewer |
| | Fowle | West St/Tanners St | |
| Thomas | Freeman | West St/Tanners St | |
| Margaret | Greenstreet | Court St West | Brewer |
| John | Harman | Abbey St West | |
| Robert | Hogben | Preston St West | Brewer |
| Roger | Hutton | Preston St West | |
| Henry | Leese | Quays | Brewer |
| Robert | Lott | ? | |
| Robert | Moore | Quays | |
| John | Newland | Court St West | |
| William | Nott | ? | |
| Widow | Taylor | ? | |
| Thomas | Upton | Court St East | Brewer |
| Dennis | Wharton | West St/Tanners St | |
| Frances | Whitehead | West St South | Brewer |
| Richard | Wild | Quays | |

Sources: *1662 Recognisenses (Licences)*
Refs: *KHLC Fa/JQr 3/2*

Table 8. *Faversham Tipplers, Alehouse Keepers, Inn Holders and Victuallers Recognisances 1691-1731*

| Year | Premises | Licencee | Status | Recog'e | Status | Recog'e | Status | Bond |
|---|---|---|---|---|---|---|---|---|
| **1691** | | | | | | | | |
| | Anchor | John Major | Victualler | Robert Lott | Victualler | Thomas Hills | Innholder | £5 |
| | Ship | Thomas Higgs | Innholder | Robert Lott | Victualler | John Major | Victualler | |
| | Dolphin | Thomas Godfrey | Victualler | Nicholas Wallard | Victualler | Thomas Clarke | Victualler | |
| | Falcon | John Collens | Victualler | William Marsh | Victualler | Mathew Denham | Victualler | |
| | Bear | Mathew Denham | Victualler | John Collens | Victualler | William Marshall | Victualler | |
| | Bull | John Thomas | Victualler | George Thomson | Victualler | Jacob Marshall | Victualler | |
| | Black Boy | Richard Wallard | Barber | Thomas Godfrey | Victualler | Thomas Clarke | Victualler | |
| | Checquer | William Catlett | Victualler | Peter Lowman | Victualler | Richard Baker | Victualler | |
| | White Horse | John Goodsold | Victualler | Benjamin Andrews | Cordwayner | William Catlett | Victualler | |
| | Castle | Richard Sherwood | Victualler | Lawrence Whatman | Cordwayner | Leonard Clarke | Grocer | |
| | George | Thomas Clarke | Victualler | Thomas Godfrey | Victualler | Nicholas Wallard | Victualler | |
| | Sun | Thomas Varham | | Daniel Wootton | Victualler | Benjamin Andrews | Cordwayner | |
| | Turks Head | John Philpot | Victualler | Edward Clarke | Grocer | Lawrence Whatman | Cordwayner | |

Table 8. *Faversham Tipplers, Alehouse Keepers, Inn Holders and Victuallers Recognisances 1691-1731 (cont.)*

| Year | Premises | Licencee | Status | Recog'e | Status | Recog'e | Status |
|---|---|---|---|---|---|---|---|
| | Mermaid | Daniel Wootton | Victualler | Thomas Varham | Victualler | Benjamin Andrews | Cordwayner |
| | Kings Head Court Street | William Marshall | Victualler | John Collens | Victualler | Mathew Denham | Victualler |
| | Blue Bell | Richard Baker | Victualler | Peter Lowman | Victualler | William Catlett | Victualler |
| | Crowne in Abbey Street | Joanna Tanner | Widow | Rosa Foreman | Widow | Dorothea Marshall | Widow |
| | Swann at Key | George Tompson | Victualler | John Thomas | Victualler | Jacob Marshall | Victualler |
| | Boatswain & Call | Rosa Foreman | Widow | Joanna Tanner | Widow | Dorothea Marshall | Widow |
| | Crowne in West Street | Peter Lowman | Victualler | Richard Baker | Victualler | William catlett | Victualler |
| | Cross Keys | Jacob Marshall | Victualler | George Thomson | Victualler | John Thomas | Victualler |
| | [Unnamed] | Elizabeth Churchman | Widow | Leonard Clarke | Grocer | Lawrence Whatman | Cordwayner |
| | Kings Head at Key | Dorothea Marshall | Widow | Joanna Tanner | Widow | Rosas Foreman | Widow |
| | Tunne | Nicholas Mockett | Victualler | John Smyth | Victualler | John Eason | Victualler |
| | Horseshoe | John Smyth | Victualler | Nicholas Wallard | Victualler | John Eason | Victualler |
| | Wheatsheafe | John Eason | Victualler | Nicholas Mockett | Victualler | John Smith | Victualler |
| | Pheasant Cocke | Benjamin Andrews | Cordwayner | Thomas Varham | Victualler | Daniel Wootton | Victualler |
| | Zurrickzee | Eva Stidall | Widow | Benjamin Andrews | Cordwayner | William Catlett | Victualler |
| | Flower de Luce | Maria Proctor | Widow | Leonard Clarke | Grocer | Lawrence Whatman | Cordwayner |
| | Masons Arms | John Berry | Cordwayner | Leonard Clarke | Grocer | John Preble | Maltster |
| **1710** | | | | | | | |
| | Three Tons | Edward Hogben | Victualler | William Harris | Victualler | Henry Marsh | Victualler |
| | Blew Anchor | Henry Marsh | Victualler | William Harris | Victualler | Edward Hogben | Victualler |
| | Ffolkon | John Vallance | Victualler | Robert Smith | Victualler | Edward Bolton | Victualler |
| | Two Brewers | Robert Smith | Victualler | John Vallance | Victualler | Thomas Bolton | Victualler |
| | Swan | Thomas Bolton | Victualler | John Vallance | Victualler | Robert Smith | Victualler |
| | Castle | Edward Seamarke | Victualler | William Catlett | Victualler | Michael Hannah | Victualler |
| | Crowne | William Catlett | Victualler | Edward Seamark | Victualler | Michael Hannah | Victualler |
| | White Horse | Michael Hannah | Victualler | William Catlet | Victualler | Edward Seamarke | Victualler |
| | Maremaid | John Hills | Victualler | Nicholas Baldocke | Victualler | William Dearne | Victualler |
| | Blew Bell | Nicholas Baldocke | Victualler | John Hills | Victualler | William Dearne | Victualler |
| | Kings Head | William Dearne | Victualler | John Hills | Victualler | Nicholas Baldocke | Victualler |
| | George | Elizabeth Miles | Widow | Yeoman Lott | Victualler | Mathew Denham | Victualler |
| | Dolphin | Yeoman Lott | Victualler | Katherine Stonestreet | Victualler | Mathew Denham | Victualler |
| | Duke of Graftons Head | Katherine Stonestreet | Widow | Yeoman Lott | Victualler | Mathew Denham | Victualler |
| | Queens Head | Richard Ashbey | Victualler | Thomas Varham | Victualler | John Gorham | Victualler |
| | Masons Arms | John Gorham | Victualler | Richard Ashbey | Victualler | Thomas Varham | Victualler |
| | Swan | Samuel Transham | Victualler | Thomas Varham | Victualler | Mathew Denham | Victualler |
| | Turks Head | Thomas Varham | Victualler | Mathew Denham | Victualler | Lawrence Whatman | Victualler |
| | Bear | Mathew Denham | Victualler | Thomas Varham | Victualler | Lawrence Whatman | Victualler |
| | Shipp | John Amis | Innholder | Thomas Varham | Victualler | Mathew Denham | Victualler |
| | [Unnamed] | Robert Packingham | Labourer | Thomas Varham | Victualler | Mathew Denham | Victualler |
| | Blackboy | Simon Brice | Victualler | Thomas Varham | Victualler | Mathew Denham | Victualler |
| | Gun | Elizabeth Marshall | Widow | Thomas Varham | Victualler | Lawrence Whatman | Victualler |
| | Gun | John Morris | Victualler | Mathew Denham | Victualler | Lawrence Whatman | Cordwayner |
| **1731** | | | | | | | |
| | Bear | Mathew Denham | Victualler | Daniel King | | Thomas Coleman | Labourer |
| | Prince of Orange Head | John Baxter | | Mathew Denham | | John Coleman | |
| | Three Tuns | Edward Knight | | Mathew Denham | | Daniel King | |
| | Two Brewers | Susanna Henman | | Joseph Whiles | Victualler | Andrew Lucas | Victualler |
| | Swann on Key | Joseph Whiles | | | | | |
| | White Hart | Andrew Lucas | | Joseph Whiles | | Edward Spillett | |
| | Mermaid | Edward Spillett | | Andrew Lucas | | Joseph Whiles | |

Table 8. *Faversham Tipplers, Alehouse Keepers, Inn Holders and Victuallers Recognisances 1691-1731 (cont.)*

| Year | Premises | Licencee | Status | Recog'e | Status | Recog'e | Status |
|---|---|---|---|---|---|---|---|
| | Castle | William Collins | | | | | |
| | Falcon | Thomas Newman | | Richard Pepper | | Thomas Kemp | |
| | Chequer | Richard Pepper | | Thomas Newman | | Thomas Kemp | |
| | Bull | John Conni | | Thomas Kemp | | John West | |
| | Sun | Thomas Kemp | | John Cony | | Thomas Newman | |
| | Dolphin | Robert Lott | | William Collins | | Thomas Newman | |
| | Kingshead | Maria Williams | | Robert Lott | | William Collins | |
| | Swan | Henry Best | | Mathew Denham | | Daniel King | |
| | Ship | Francis Hunt | Victualler | Mathew Denham | | Daniel King | |
| | Gun | Martha Morris | | Mathew Denham | | Daniel King | |
| | White Horse | Eliza Hanna | | Mathew Denham | | Daniel King | |
| | Blue Anchor | Maria Ellen | | Daniel King | | John Coleman | |
| | Queens Head | Margaret Bereling | | Mathew Denham | | Daniel King | |
| | Black Moor Head | Margaret Varham | | Mathew Denham | | Daniel King | |
| | Black Boy | Eliza Brice | | Mathew Denham | | John Coleman | |
| | Ship | Eliza Hodges | | Mathew Denham | | Daniel King | |
| | Masons Arms | Richard Lewsby | | Mathew Denham | | Daniel King | |
| | Bell | Richard Daniel | | Mathew Denham | | Daniel King | |

Source: *Recognisances (Licences)*
Ref: *KHLC. Fa JQr 2*

Table 9. *Faversham Population and Estimated Barrelage 1327-1732*

| Year | Population Estimate England | Inner London Former London County | Faversham | Villages | Combined | Barrelage Consumption per Annum |
|---|---|---|---|---|---|---|
| 1327 | 3.5m | 45,000 | 1450 | 390 | 1840 | 13985 |
| 1400 | 2.25m | | 950 | 255 | 1205 | 9160 |
| 1500 | 2.5m | | 1050 | 280 | 1330 | 10110 |
| 1550 | 3.2m | | 1300 | 350 | 1650 | 12540 |
| 1600 | 4m | 200,000 | 1650 | 445 | 2095 | 15920 |
| 1650 | 5m | 400,000 | 2050 | 550 | 2600 | 19760 |
| 1700 | 5m | 600,000 | 2050 | 550 | 2600 | 19760 |
| 1725 | 5.5m | 625,000 | 2250 | 610 | 2860 | 21740 |
| 1801 | 8.5m | 950,000 | 3490 | 950 | 4440 | |

Sources: *Wrigley & Schofield. Population of England.*
*1801 Census*
*Est. Average Consumption 0.75 Gallons per Day per Person*
*(7.6 Barrels per Year per Person)*
*Villages: Preston, Ospringe & Davington*
*Faversham and Villages Populations based on back projection from 1801*

# Pedigrees

PEDIGREE of the Family of CASTLOCKE of Faversham

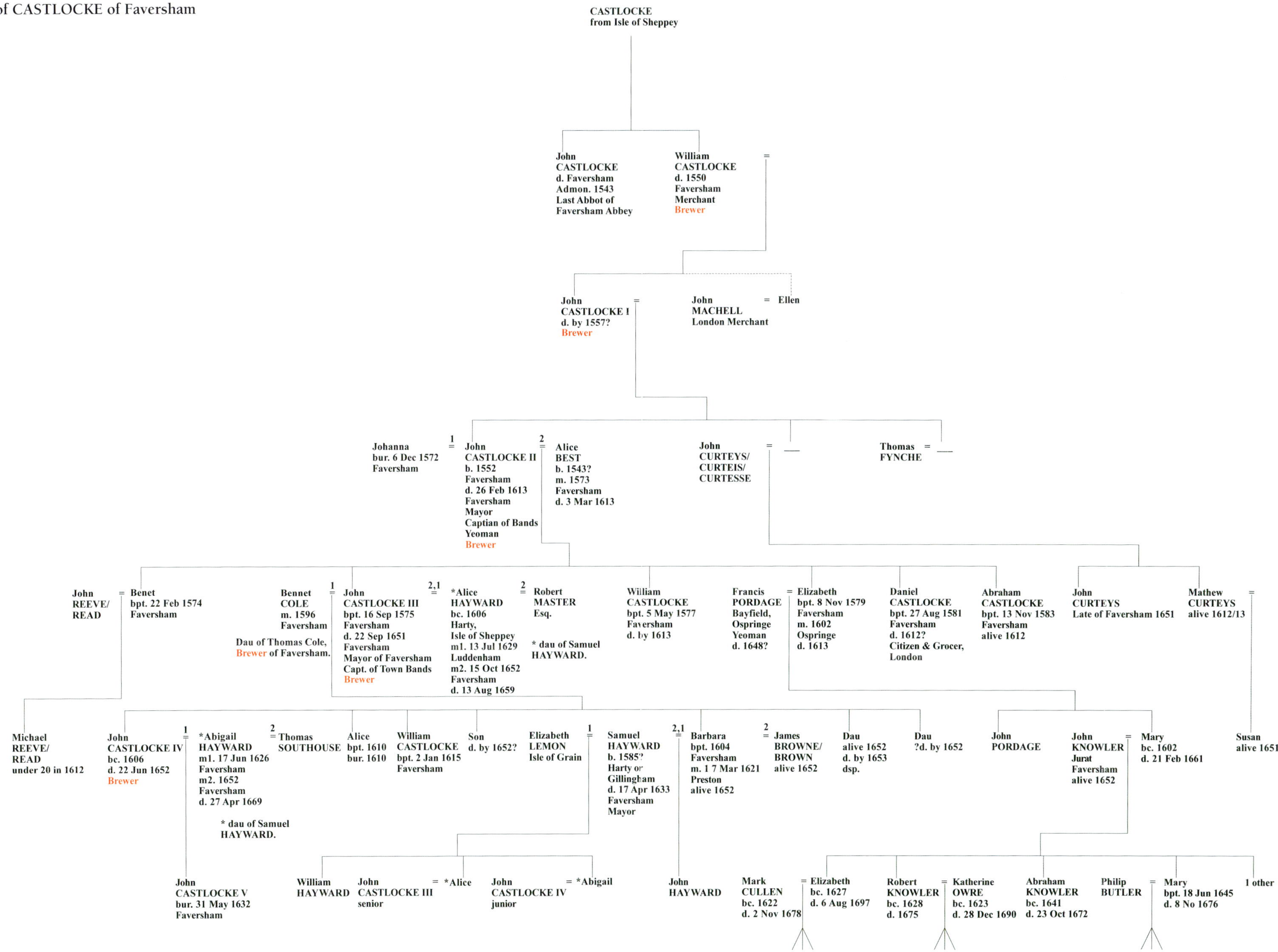

PEDIGREE of Family of MARSH of Faversham and Womenswold Kent

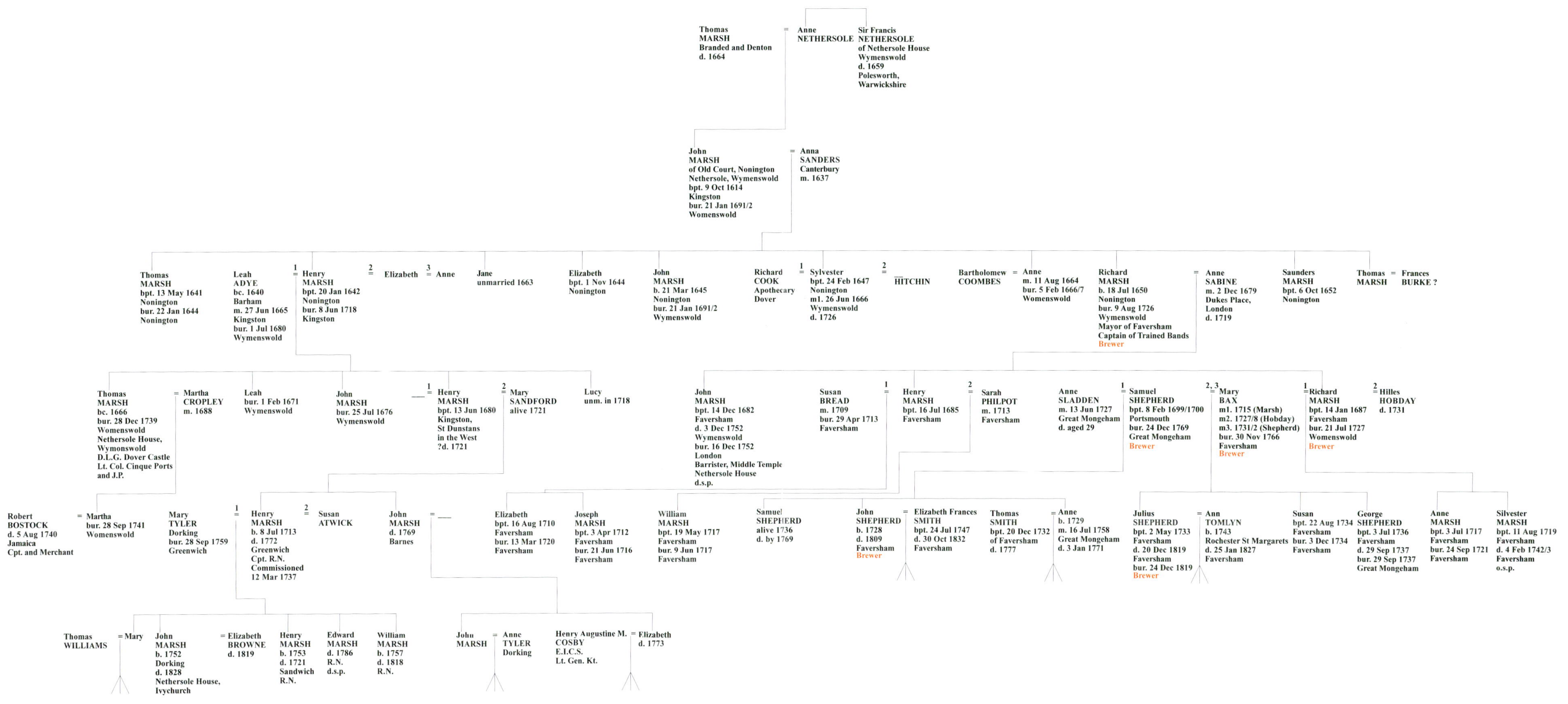

# Index

## A



## B

# C



# D



# E

# F



# G

# H



# I



# J



# K



# L



# M

# N



# O



# P

# U



# V



# W



# Y